11 5⁰/10 AC

D0126848

DISCARDED

THE DILEMMA OF AMERICAN MUSIC

AND OTHER ESSAYS

By DANIEL GREGORY MASON

BEETHOVEN AND HIS FORERUNNERS
THE ROMANTIC COMPOSERS
FROM GRIEG TO BRAHMS: STUDIES
    OF SOME MODERN COMPOSERS
CONTEMPORARY COMPOSERS

THE DILEMMA OF AMERICAN MUSIC

AND OTHER ESSAYS

BY

DANIEL GREGORY MASON

GREENWOOD PRESS, PUBLISHERS
NEW YORK

Copyright © 1928 by the Macmillan Company

Reprinted by permission
of the Macmillan Company

First Greenwood Reprinting, 1969

Library of Congress Catalogue Card Number 69-13989

SBN 8371-1155-2

PRINTED IN UNITED STATES OF AMERICA

PREFACE

It is hoped that these essays are worth reprinting for whatever light they throw on certain questions, chiefly of our contemporary musical situation, which, important as they are, are also highly puzzling, and not likely to be soon settled. The first eight deal with problems of present-day music, especially in America. They are addressed to that large body of intelligent listeners—neither "highbrows" nor "low-brows," but plain men and women,—who must contribute their active cooperation to our American musical art if it is really to live. To these are added four papers on more general topics, particularly the important and neglected matter of rhythm, five on Beethoven, and a brief epilogue of which perhaps the moral is that music in America is after all just music.

Criticisms brought forth by the essay on our orchestras have persuaded the writer that it is in some ways misleading. "Moronic conservatives" are probably less numerous than it suggests. Certainly their menace to our musical

697000

health is far less than that of "moronic radicals," with their unintelligent clamor for ceaseless novelty, reverberated by box-office and press. The essay hardly does justice to what it calls the museum function of an orchestra—its prime business of presenting the great music of the world to the general public, not to specialists, professionals, or sensation-seekers. This service is so indispensable that possibly a division of the laboratory and the museum functions in separate orchestras may eventually prove the best means of adjusting the claims of old and new. Despite these grave defects of proportion and emphasis, the paper is allowed to stand in the hope that it may provoke further discussion of a problem of increasing seriousness in our musical life.

For permission to reprint, grateful acknowledgment is made: to the *American Mercury* for "The Dilemma of American Music" and "Stravinsky as a Symptom"; to *The Freeman* for "Music and the Plain Man," "Vincent d'Indy in America," and "The Paradox of Beethoven"; to the *Musical Quarterly* for "The Depreciation of Music"; to the *Virginia Quarterly Review* for "Sensationalism and Indifference"; to *Harper's Magazine* for "Our

Orchestras and Our Money's Worth"; to *The New Music Review* for "Two Critics of Ultramodernism" and "The Tyranny of the Barline"; to *Musical America* for "A Note on English Rhythms"; to *The Nation* for "How Beethoven Worked"; to the *Detroit Symphony Orchestra Program-books* for "Beethoven's Humor" and part of "Reflections on Rhythm"; to the *Columbia Phonograph Company* for the Centennial Essay "Beethoven: 1827-1927"; and to *The Arts* for "Reflections on Rhythm," "Beethoven: 1770-1920," and "Three Restaurants." "Creative Leisure" is reprinted from an address delivered at Columbia University, in September, 1928.

D. G. M.

32 Via dell'Erta Canina,
Florence, June, 1928.

CONTENTS

THE DILEMMA OF
AMERICAN MUSIC

AND OTHER ESSAYS

THE DILEMMA OF
AMERICAN MUSIC

I

ALTHOUGH it is impossible nowadays to
mention American music without hearing someone murmur, as if in echo, "jazz,"
there is, as a matter of fact, a great deal
more in the best American music of our day
than "pep," "punch," and "kick," and we have
a number of composers, of competent technical skill and distinctive personality, who have
no commerce with the ragtime jerk. American music, indeed, is already a sturdy offshoot
of the great tree of European music, and sufficiently flourishing to deserve respectful attention. No doubt the work of even our best
composers still leaves something to be de-
sired, for they labor under great impediments,
chiefly psychological; but they have given us
nevertheless a music, and a music that is not
jazz.

Perhaps it would be better to say that they
have given us ten or a dozen musics. It is
highly characteristic of their situation that instead of working in one clear tradition, as

their German, French, or Italian brothers more or less do, they are bewildered by the multiplicity of the traditions which with us subsist side by side, mutually diluting, confusing, or even cancelling one another. This confusion of tradition is a peculiarity of American artistic life. If anyone thinks it a small or an academic matter, let him consider for a moment how large a proportion of all that is finest in the musical art of the world owes its existence to tradition: how much of Bach's style, for instance, is reflected directly from his predecessors; how impossible Beethoven would have been without Haydn and Mozart, or Wagner without Meyerbeer and Weber; how fully are already present in Beethoven the germs of Schubert and Schumann, and in them those of Brahms and César Franck.

To consider these things is to get a sense of how small is even the greatest individual, how all-determining is the tradition he works in. Weissmann asks what would have happened to Mozart had he been born in the Samoan Islands, what he would have been able to do. At most, he thinks, he might have extended the native gamut of three or four tones to seven, and created melodies a little

2

more complicated; but "he would have been as incapable of composing symphonies as Archimedes would have been to invent an electric dynamo." Art is a coral reef, and the greatest artist is only one more insect, owing his virtue more to his attachments than to himself. Hence it is no small matter that there is in American music no main reef, but only a confusion of tendencies. With us even the most gifted individuals find it difficult to attach themselves anywhere; instead, they swim distractedly about, make head-on collisions, and generally get in one another's way.

II

The first of all our traditions,—indeed, for a long time the only one that powerfully affected us—was that of German romanticism. Roughly speaking, it dominated our music from its first timid beginnings about 1850 until, let us say, 1890. Those of us who studied with the first serious American composer in the larger forms, Professor John Knowles Paine of Harvard, remember how submissively his music reflected the romanticism of Schumann and Mendelssohn, just as most of the American literature of that period re-

flected English models. His "Island Fantasy"
was supposed to be inspired by the Isles of
Shoals, off Portsmouth, but artistically speaking it was within easy sailing distance of Mendelssohn's "Hebrides."

His younger colleagues and followers, Arthur Foote and George W. Chadwick, did valuable work, but belong on the whole, like him,
to the epoch when our music was dominated
by German models. MacDowell was of the
same heredity, his line coming out of Schumann
through Joachim Raff. His greater distinction came largely from his narrower assimi-
lativeness, and was purchased at a price. Three
Rheinberger pupils contributed much to our
music: Henry Holden Huss, a composer of
unusual romantic charm but inadequate constructive and self-critical power; Arthur Whiting, one of our most genuinely native talents
despite the meagerness of his output, and Ho-
ratio Parker, so facile and so voluminous, and
on the whole so characterless. Then there is
Edgar Stillman Kelley, whose "New England
Symphony," technically one of the most competent works our country has produced, is German to the backbone. Despite its title, there
is in it scarcely more of New England than

4

there is of Old England in the works of Bennett, MacFarren, and other composers of the period when England was dominated by Handel and Mendelssohn. Like most of the works of its generation it is, as Mr. Arthur Whiting once called the songs of a young American composer, "as German as kraut." In most of these works the dominance of a foreign model seems to paralyse personal feeling. MacDowell is almost the only exception, and he purchased individuality at the price of a terrible limitation of style and emotional reach.

The first powerful rival influence to that of Germany, beginning to make itself felt about 1890, came from France, quickened to national self-consciousness by the Franco-Prussian war. It assumed two strongly contrasted forms: first, the modification of romantic sentiment toward the classic reserve, balance, and plastic beauty naturally produced by French love of clearness and order, as manifested in the work of César Franck and his greatest disciple, Vincent d'Indy; second, the distrust of all sentiment and the devotion to sensuous charm typically represented by the impressionism of Debussy and the irony of Ravel. Some of us who were in college in the nineties found the mys-

5

ticism and spirituality of Franck and d'Indy quite as potently persuasive as the less subtle romanticism of Schumann and Brahms, and were irresistibly led to try to incorporate in our style both streams of influence. Others were more attracted by the novelty of the sensuous appeal of the impressionists, who enjoyed moreover an infinitely greater vogue.

Debussy and Ravel are reflected in such contemporary American composers as Edward Burlingame Hill and John Alden Carpenter, both of whom studied under Paine at Harvard in the nineties, as unmistakably as Schumann and Raff are reflected in MacDowell. Hill, as he has shown in his orchestral suite, "Stevensoniana," can score with a richness and clarity of color evidently learned at the feet of the French impressionists, though combined with a naïveté and tenderness of feeling quite personal. In other works, such as "The Fall of the House of Usher," he is less personal, more conventional, more purely reflective. Many of Carpenter's clever and refined—almost too refined—songs and piano pieces might have been written by Debussy, while his Suite for orchestra, "Adventures in a Perambulator," is essen-

6

tially Gallic in its economy of means, its distinctiveness of color, and its ironic wit.

Of all the cases of French influence no doubt the most striking is that of Charles Martin Loeffler. Alsatian by birth, something of an exotic in America, Loeffler is surely one of our most distinguished composers, distinguished especially through the singleness and complete unity of his style, entirely French in its fastidious reticence, its refinement of sentiment and its delicacy of color. And what is more, he is not only exclusively French, but inclusively French: there is in his string quartet in memory of Victor Chapman, for instance, the noble seriousness and earnest though reticent feeling of d'Indy, and there is, in works like the "Pagan Poem" for orchestra, the sensuous fascination of Debussy. Such works are as fine as anything that modern France itself has produced.

III

At the end of the nineteenth century, then, two traditions dominated our American music, both imported, one from Germany, the other from France. Those composers who through singleness of temperament and concentration of mind succeeded in thoroughly assimilating one tradition and one only, as MacDowell did German romanticism and Loeffler did French impressionism, succeeded in producing works that still have a life of their own, however narrow, and a permanent artistic validity.

During the first quarter of the twentieth century, however, when traditions began to multiply among us with alarming rapidity, such concentration became more and more difficult to achieve. We must remember that one does not master a tradition merely by defining it academically or understanding it intellectually; one has to live into it, to make it by long habit a part of one's point of view; and the more traditions one is sensitive to, and the more various and perhaps even opposed they are, the more arduous is this assimilation. We have had from the beginning, unfortunately, too many parrot composers, clever enough in imitating any prevalent idiom of musical speech, but too superficial to ponder its meaning. Our path is littered with still-born "masterpieces," once acclaimed and now forgotten. The more traditions there are to follow the more featureless does such an eclecticism become; and

8

in our day the traditions have become so
tangled that only the most powerful intelli-
gences can find their way through them, only
the simplest spirits can proceed undismayed
by them to the goals appointed by their
temperaments.

There were, for instance, several minor national traditions which, though far less powerful than the German and the French, began
to make definite claims upon our attention.
There was what we may call Russian barbarism, which came to us from Moussorgsky
and Rimsky-Korsakoff, via Prokofieff and
Stravinsky. Leo Ornstein was the chief American composer, if such he may be called, to
listen to that formidable Amazonian siren.
Then the torrid sunlight of subtropical Spain
was flashed into our cooler atmosphere by
Albeniz, Granados, and others, and reflected
for our dazzlement by Ernest Schelling. Musical speech began to fall upon our ears in many
strange and outlandish dialects. Grieg beguiled us with a Norwegian accent, Dvořák
with a Bohemian, Sibelius with a Northern
wail, Elgar with a bit of British drawl, and
Stanford with a brogue. Quick to take a hint,
we began to exploit our own "local color," and

blossomed forth in Indian suites and Negro rhapsodies.

Once started, the process of differentiation did not stop with nationalism, but began to produce many conflicting schools, groups, and cliques. In Europe itself music, already decadent in the preciousness and exaggerated sensuousness of Debussy and in the distrust of its own feelings betrayed by the irony of Ravel, lost unity and balance altogether, and broke into fragments. Differentiation became disintegration. Musicians ranged themselves in rival camps, all more or less partial and futile. In one were pedants like Reger and Schönberg, trying to ratiocinate their way to a beauty that comes only through feeling. In another were hysterics like Scriabine, striving to refine the soul of art out of its body. In still another were the impatient and the disillusioned, who like irritable children smashed the toys they could not mend (the Italian *bruiteurs*, for instance), or who, like the Dadaists or French Group of Six, finding reality too slow, exacting, and laborious for them, reverted to infantility and took to riding rocking-horses.

At the very moment of this disintegration in Europe, we in America, through the economic effects of the war, were put more than ever into the position of a receiver nation. Already before the war we looked to Europe for guidance with all the conscious inferiority of youth and inexperience; now, without increasing our wisdom, the war vastly increased our power, by placing Europe in the relation to us of bankrupt parents forced to defer to immature children in order to live. Since 1914 musicians of every country on earth have flowed in upon us in an unending stream. The music of the whole world has battered our ears. For us, the only ones with wherewithal to pay the piper, the habitable globe has danced and sung.

How could we hope to stand against such a flood? What was there for us to do but open our mouths and shut our eyes, and try to swallow as much of it all as we could without drowning? Too much passive reception, too little self-realising activity—that had always been the characteristic danger of our situation. Under the vast mass and variety of influences that now swept in upon us our modest powers of assimilation were hopelessly deluged and gutted. We became vast stomachs to swallow at one gulp the music of the universe, while

our legs and arms, just timidly sprouting, gave
up the unequal struggle and withered away.
In short, American music from 1914 to 1928
is the Music of Indigestion.

Go to a concert of any of the "advanced"
organisations of the day, such as the International Composers' Guild, and listen to the rum-
blings and belchings of this indigestion.
Listen to the confusion worse confounded of
our house of a hundred traditions, our modern
Babel. Hear Emerson Whithorne's Chinese
tunes, as insulated in their European harmonies as the inhabitants of Pell Street in modern New York. Watch Samuel Gardner's
Russian folk-song bacteria bombinating in a
matrix vapidly German-sentimentalist. Study
Henry F. Gilbert's negroes in his "Comedy
Overture on Negro Themes": not full-blooded,
you will observe, but half-breeds—quadroons
—octoroons—descended by some repellent
miscegenation from Beethoven and Mendelssohn. Notice Charles Wakefield Cadman's
Indians, whose only arrows are collars from
Troy, and who wear derby hats. Even John
Powell, the most gifted of all our "folk" com-
posers, apparently does not recoil when, in his
"Rhapsodie Nègre" (French titles have ap-

pealed to American composers ever since the days of Gottschalk) the swarthy faces of his protagonists suddenly assume the Jesuitical smile of Liszt.

Alas, the confusion of traditions among us is disastrously bewildering, even to the greatest talents. We are not only parrots, but polyglot parrots. Where shall we recapture our native tongue, or at least learn to speak the Esperanto of cosmopolitanism with voices recognisably our own and an authority not borrowed? This has become the insistent æsthetic question of the day, upon our finding a right answer to which seems to depend our artistic salvation.

IV

One answer which has attracted much attention, both by the plausibility of its theory and by the interest of practical results already obtained, is that of the nationalists. It is based on the analogy of the various national awakenings that have taken place in European music, such as that of Germany, throwing off the yoke of Italian opera in the work of Mozart, Weber, and Wagner: of France, finding itself in the activities of the *Société Nationale*

and other organisations and individuals after
1870: of Russia, reaching national self-consciousness in Borodine, Moussorgsky, and Rimsky-Korsakoff: and finally of England, assert-
ing itself only in our own day through the work
of Vaughan Williams, Gustav Holst and other
living composers.

This last nationalism, that of England, is
quite naturally, and for several reasons, the
one that has most deeply impressed us here in
America. It is not only the most recent but
the nearest, since we are conscious of a closer
kinship with the English, æsthetically, tempera-
mentally, and socially, than with any European
people. Moreover, exactly the same kind of
featureless eclecticism that has blighted so much
of our own music was imposed on England for
generations by the prestige of Handel and Mendelssohn; and to hear at last Elgar, Holst, and
Vaughan Williams after so many Sterndale
Bennetts, Cowens, MacFarrens, and Prouts,
fills us with a great hope. In this we
have been encouraged by observant visitors.
Vaughan Williams himself did not hesitate to
prophesy, after his first visit to us, that we
should go through the same evolution as England. We were about a generation behind the

14

mother country, he told us; our present men were doing the educational and preparatory work accomplished there by Parry, Stanford, and their fellows; and in twenty-five years we might hope to see such a school of native composers as flourishes there now.

English nationalism is undeniably a vital movement. No doubt its claims may be sometimes exaggerated, as the claims of all nationalisms seem to have a way of being; we may see reasons, as we go on, for questioning the universal applicability of its theory, and the exclusive validity of its practice, especially under other conditions. But that it has breathed new life into English music in the last twenty years seems certain. The extraordinary beauty and variety of the native songs and dances of Britain were first revealed through the work of enthusiasts like Cecil Sharp, who devoted a laborious life to discovering, recording, arranging, and publishing them. Through the British Folk-Song Society, founded by Sharp, they were given wide vogue. Attractive settings of them were made by many composers, slightly elaborated but preserving their essential naïveté.

Interest quickly spread from them to the less

15

popular, more artistic music of early England, and such labors as Fellowes' monumental collection of sixteenth century madrigals revealed an undreamed-of richness in the native musical background. Scholars began to discuss the melodic, modal, and rhythmic peculiarities of this music, and composers more or less consciously to mold their style upon it. The result was what may fairly be called a new voice in the chorus of the world's music. Such works as Vaughan Williams's "Variations on a Theme of Thomas Tallis" and his "London" and "Pastoral Symphonies" are as unmistakably English as d'Indy's "Symphony on a Mountain Song" is French, or Balakireff's "Islamey" Russian. Vaughan Williams has carried the same methods into opera in his "Hugh the Drover," in which, appropriately enough, the hero fights the villain not with sword or poniard but with good British fists; and Holst has woven an entire one-act opera, "At the Boar's Head," out of thirty-odd traditional tunes.

Meanwhile Sharp himself was carrying his investigations into America, discovering in the Appalachian Mountains and other rural districts little affected by civilisation many survivals of songs brought from England genera-

tions ago. His publications contain curious examples of songs less corrupted by time in America than in England, or differently corrupted
here, just as our speech is said to preserve Eliza-
bethan words obsolete in their native land.
Howard Brockway in his two collections,
"Songs of the Kentucky Mountains" and
"Lonesome Tunes" (as these melodies are
quaintly called by the mountaineers) has made
available much material of great historic interest and, what is better, refreshing artistic simplicity and charm. Both Brockway and Leo
Sowerby have made folk-music settings as attractive as those of Percy Grainger, and David
Guion has given us in "Turkey in the Straw" as
fetching and as Anglo-Saxon a dance as "Shep-
herd's Hey" itself. So far as the larger forms
are concerned our composers have been slower
to venture on the new ground. John Powell is
almost the only one who has as yet worked
there successfully, in such pieces as his "Sonata
Virginianesque," his Violin Concerto, and
above all his orchestral overture, "In Old Virginia." This work is American-English in the
sense in which Vaughan Williams's "Pastoral
Symphony" is English-English; and in its own
way it is as beautiful.

17

Is it necessary, however, we are likely to find ourselves asking at this point, that all of our music in America should be of this American-English variety? Is it indeed even desirable? Why should not some of our American music be American-German (from Pennsylvania), or American-French (from New Orleans), or American-Jewish (from New York), or even American-Negro or Red Indian? May it not be, in fact, that a nationalistic theory which works out well enough for a tight little island like England, or even for the four tight little islands of Britain, must find itself all at sea (if one may mix metaphors in describing a very mixed situation) in a melting-pot such as our modern America? May it not be that we are necessarily polyglot, and that to speak American, in any comprehensive sense, is to speak, not English, but something rather more resembling the language of the Swiss tourist: *"Donnez-moi some aqua calda, bitte"*? In any department of life the Nordic is a sufficiently absurd figment of theory; in music, with its deep obligations to Italians, Germans, Frenchmen, and Jews, and its power of leaping all barriers of race and of class, he is likely to be both ridiculous and pernicious. The nationalistic

18

thread hardly seems capable of leading us very far, then, in such a labyrinth as we inhabit.

V

But since in art practice is always more important than theory, the theoretical difficulties of nationalism in America, obvious as they are, come to seem formidable only when we consider certain practical results of all efforts to apply it

Figure I

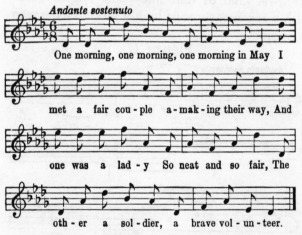

Andante sostenuto

One morning, one morning, one morning in May I met a fair cou-ple a-mak-ing their way, And one was a lad-y So neat and so fair, The oth-er a sol-dier, a brave vol-un-teer.

to our music. It seems to be a formula so narrow that it can hardly be applied without being broken. Thus if we observe carefully

the work of a folk-music setter such as Brockway or Grainger, we find that he can never quite
accept the narrow limits of the idiom he is
using; we notice that he constantly passes beyond the tradition of his material, and enhances
its interest by features borrowed from other traditions and wider ones; and if we have a keen
sense of style we feel a resultant incongruity.

When Brockway prefaces a forthright *do-re-
mi-fa-sol* kind of tune like "The Nightingale"
with a few measures of highly subtle Debussyan
harmonies,

Figure II

when Grainger buries the lithe body of an Irish melody

Figure III

under fold on fold of Wagnerian velvet and brocade,

Figure IV

we are delighted, but uncomfortable; we feel
that something is wrong; it is like being sum-
moned to dinner in the sonorous sentences of
Sir Thomas Browne. When, on the other hand,
a composer manfully accepts the restrictions
of folk-song idiom, and harmonises, as does
Vaughan Williams in his "Pastoral Symphony,"
page after page with nothing but triads moving
en masse, as if clamped together,

Figure V

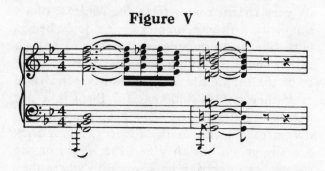

we grow uneasy for another reason; monotony skirts the edge of boredom, and limits begin to seem like limitations. The difficulty that all nationalists seem to find in sailing a course that will avoid shipwreck either on the Scylla of incongruity or the Charybdis of bareness seems to suggest a fatal defect in their idiom itself. It seems to be so primitive, melodically, harmonically, and structurally, in comparison with other idioms with which we are all perfectly familiar, that it will neither mix with them naturally nor long hold our interest without them.

Our sense of restriction in the idiom of folksong seems, moreover, to be but the index of a deeper dissatisfaction we cannot but feel in its emotional and intellectual poverty. No doubt its very charm comes from the contrast of its simplicity with our complexity; no doubt beings born like us to complexity are apt to have a rather morbid craving for what they imagine to be the simple life; but when they get a taste of it they always find that for them it is not natural but artificial. City people often day-dream of a picnic in the country; but if they actually go on one they find that much of the charm lies in getting back again to where they feel at home. Modern music-lovers may enjoy a folk-song or dance for a change, but for a steady diet they find a Brahms symphony or a Wagner music-drama more satisfying than the Volga Boat-song or "Barbara Allen." Whatever the faddists may say, the world of folk music is really too narrow a habitat for us to feel comfortable in; to live in it is for us unnatural. Says Ernest Newman: "The nationalists isolate a certain genre of expression—the folk-music of centuries ago—and tell us that only by absorbing this genre into his tissues can an English composer hope to be English. That, I claim, is a monstrous fallacy. A modern novel- who sees the life around him imaginatively clearly can make first-rate English art out of what he sees, even if he has never read a single old English legend or heard a single old English ballad. The composer has only to do what the novelist does. If he feels deeply and sincerely about life, and can find beautiful and convincing expression for what he and the rest of us living people feel, he will make great English art even though he may never have heard a folk-song and never have seen an agricultural laborer."

Thus when we examine closely the claims of nationalism it seems to fail us, at least as a universal formula. Even in England, where the mixture of nations and of races and the confusion of traditions is so much less than here, nationalism is prevented from being a universal panacea by its intrinsic limitations both of idiom and of emotional and intellectual scope. We seem therefore to be thrown back upon eclecticism, and obliged to ask whether there is not, after all, some other kind of eclecticism than the "featureless" variety. May there not be also an eclecticism of power, of choice, of individuality? May not the distinctiveness achievable by American composers be a personal rather than a national distinctiveness? May not such personal distinctiveness be, indeed, the only kind that is genuinely attainable in an art that has reached such complexity and cosmopolitanism as modern music?

This view, to be sure, cannot hope to be agreeable to our American taste for herding, for standardising, for doing everything in large numbers and *en masse*. But in art no formula can be universal, and it is precisely the pretension of nationalism to universality that is its most injurious trait. Nationalism is excellent as an ingredient, but disastrous as a dogma. The promising way towards a rich and various American music seems much less likely to lie through any system of branding, organising, and licensing, such as nationalism and all other "isms" are too apt to foster, than through an elastic eclecticism of individual choice.

Originality has been well defined by Van Wyck Brooks as "a capacity to survive and surmount experience after having met and assimilated it." If he is right there must be possible to us as many musical personalities as there are possible combinations and permutations of vital traditions. Therefore, when Mac-Dowell meets and assimilates German romanticism, when Loeffler meets and assimilates French impressionism, when Powell meets and assimilates Anglo-American folk-song, let us

26

not cavil and define, let us rather rejoice and applaud. Were a single one of them to be forcibly "Americanised," music in America would be the poorer. Music in America is the richer for each and all of them; and music in America is a thing far more worth working for than "American music."

MUSIC AND THE PLAIN MAN

I

O NLY observers deluded by the systematic
optimism, the "hurrah-boys" attitude of
so much of our American opinion, can believe
that all is for the best with our music, in the
best of possible worlds. It may be true, as
we are so constantly reminded, that we spend
more millions of dollars on music than any
other nation, but the question still remains:
Do we get good value for our money? In
other words, is our musical life satisfactory
not only to our financial pride but to our emotional and æsthetic sense? Is it wide and deep
and pervasive, free of fads on the one hand and
crudity on the other? Does it solace as well as
divert us? The answer must be, one fears,
either a negative one or a highly qualified af-
firmative. The lack of breadth, solidarity,
pervasiveness in our musical life is only too apparent to any candid observer. It does not
range freely up and down through our whole
society, but separates into layers, a thin froth

at the top, dregs at the bottom, and, to let the metaphor have its way, very little that is either nourishing or refreshing where the beer ought to be. In other words, the "high-brows" and the "low-brows" divide our music between them; the plain man has no use for it, and leaves it severely alone, much to his own loss, and to that of music. What are the reasons for this neglect, either contemptuous or bashful, of music by the plain man, and what hopeful signs are there that it may be modified?

In the widest, most general terms it may be said that in all periods it has been the amateur spirit, the personal love for music and personal effort to participate in making it, with whatever technical limitations, that has brought the plain man and music together; and that, on the other hand, it has been the professional spirit, the regard for high technical finish above æsthetic emotion, the contempt for limitations and imperfections, that have separated them. It was the love of singing among plain people that sustained Bach; it was the violin- and violoncello-playing gentlemen of the Esterhazy and other courts who inspired Haydn's string quartets; it was the wide diffusion of musical feeling among Austrians who themselves sang

29

and played that made Beethoven possible. We Americans, on the other hand, live in an age and country that rank science far above art, we take the efficiency expert as our model of the god-like, we are distrustful and impatient of all limitations, all imperfections, all individual irregularities, and tirelessly seek to "standardise" or "organise" them out of existence.[1] Hence among us the life-giving amateur spirit has largely succumbed to large-scale production under professional expert direction. The dangers of such a course, it is true, have begun to arouse our critics. Such books as "Babbitt" and "Main Street," such plays as "R. U. R.," "The World We Live In," and "The Adding Machine," have begun to show us the horrors of a world in which individualism and the amateur spirit have been crushed by machinery and the herd. Movements toward a more free, individual, and joyous creative activity have spontaneously arisen in several fields, notably in the theater. They begin to appear, somewhat uncertainly, in music.

One can easily imagine how one of the most significant of such movements, that towards

[1] See "Artistic Ideals," by Daniel Gregory Mason, especially the essays on "Independence" and "Workmanship."

more and better choral singing, both in college glee clubs and in more adult groups, might be regarded by a typical efficiency-expert. Why on earth, he might ask us pityingly, should we try to revive so primitive an instrument as the human voice, an instrument of a miserable octave or two of range, which trembles, which quavers, which most precariously even holds the pitch, in a scientific age that has given us such perfect and powerful engines as the mechanical piano, the phonograph (with megaphone attachment), and radio? We might as well exchange our high-powered cars for ox-carts, our rapid-firing guns for bows and arrows, our incandescent bulbs for guttering candles. We live in an age compared with which that of Beethoven is barbarous, primitive, childish. We can produce music in quantity, accurately standardised, overwhelmingly sonorous, and distributable to a thousand centers at once. We can do all this, and yet we are not satisfied. We want to sing!

Yes, we want to sing; there can be no doubt about that. Although it is not long since the Harvard Glee Club, bravely pioneering under the guidance of Dr. Archibald T. Davison, showed us that college men can sing good music, and sing it stirringly well, already these sounds, so novel to a generation accustomed to being serenaded only by "Bullfrogs on the Bank," are being reëchoed in swelling chorus from California, Columbia, Leland Stanford, Princeton, and other colleges the country over. We have seen the extraordinary spectacle of the Harvard Glee Club making a concert tour in France, and at home joining well-known symphony orchestras in producing classic masterpieces. We have seen ten college glee clubs of thirty men each participating in intercollegiate singing competitions in Carnegie Hall, New York. We have even seen the movement spread from the colleges to the preparatory schools, so that our boys are by way of being trained from early years to participate actively in the production of good music by the oldest and most fundamental of all instruments, the voice.

Similarly, we want to play; convincing proof of that is the growth of school, settlement, and college orchestras. Pioneers like Glenn H. Woods of Oakland, California, have done wonders in developing the possibilities of instrumental music in educational institutions, both practically and theoretically. Harvard, Yale, and Columbia have long had their student orchestras, of which the Pierian Sodality at Harvard is the prototype; and now their example is being followed by most colleges, and even high schools, in large cities, and indeed by many even of the grade schools. Mrs. Satis N. Coleman, in her book, "Creative Music for Children," tells how she has set the smallest children to ensemble playing, on instruments of their own manufacture. At the same time the settlements are doing invaluable work in giving lessons on instruments to those who will be the future members of the high school and college groups. A striking instance of the educative value of all this activity may be cited from Columbia. The college Glee Club, dissatisfied with the trivial music rendered by the Mandolin Club, its associate in concert tours, separated from it by a process denominated by Dean Hawkes as "divorce without alimony." At the same time, undergraduate sentiment expressed itself clearly in favor of an orchestra of less primitive instruments than mandolins, to play better music. In all such cases, the initiative comes, to a surprising degree, from the undergraduates themselves.

Now if the efficiency-expert is right in regard

to the technical superiority of professional and
machine-made music, what justification have we
for welcoming this singing and playing of amateurs as a good omen? This is a question to
be answered only by calling attention to a distinction that we have sadly neglected in America during the last twenty or thirty years. We
must distinguish between our capacity as con-
sumers, in which we want the best music that
money can buy, and our activity as producers,
which is primarily educative or taste-formative,
in which the quality of the product is of secondary importance, but the intimateness of the
process is capital. We rightly judge professional music from the point of view of the con-
sumer; but amateur music must be judged from
that of the producer. Psychologically, the act
of doing the thing oneself, however crudely
and stumblingly, gives one an insight into it
that one can never get by hiring someone else
to do it. To one who does not feel his own
way into it, it will never become alive. Our
national timidity in artistic matters, our fear of
making fools of ourselves by individual activity
before the herd, our superstitious reverence for
great names and reputations, and above all
for great prices, have cheated us out of count-

34

less humble activities that would have given us
untold joy. As an Englishman once put it:
"You Americans hire singers from the Metropolitan Opera House to entertain you of an
evening, instead of singing, dancing, or playing, according to your talents, as we do in
England, to amuse yourselves."

II

Particularly fatal to our amateur activities
has been the inhuman technical superiority of
the mechanical instrument, a sort of super-pro-
fessional. The credit side of our account with
the "musical Ford" or "horseless pianoforte,"
as Mr. Arthur Whiting calls it,[2] is so easily
discernible, and has been so tirelessly set forth
by the writers of advertisements, that it needs
no mention here. It is the debit side, particularly as it affects the amateur and his taste-
forming activities, that has been neglected. Mr.
Whiting, the most convincing as well as by far
the most amusing devil's advocate who has pre-
sented a brief in the matter, begins by describing an average musical family, in which "Sister
has a sweet touch, and Father shares, sympa-

[2] "The Mechanical Player," by Arthur Whiting. *Yale Review,* July, 1919.

35

thetically, her struggle to round out a phrase, for although he does not know it, their combined effort is a part of the emotional experience." To this humble paradise, enter a serpent in the shape of a pianola. Mr. Whiting describes it in unforgettable sentences:

They all stand before the just-arrived mechanical player, which, being entirely self-possessed, has even more platform imperturbability than the applauded virtuoso, even a larger number of decorations on its chest from the hands of grateful sovereigns, is as well set up and as shiny, exhaling a delicate odor of the varnish of its native warerooms. After a few introductory sounds which have nothing to do with the music, and without relaxing the lines of its inscrutable face, the insensate artist proceeds to show its power. Its security puts all hand-playing to shame; it never hesitates, it surmounts the highest difficulties without changing a clutch. Always masterful and headlong, it can, if required, utter notes faster than the human ear can follow. Bouquets of adjectives, thrown by the excited audience towards the unperspiring, unexhausted performer, fall unnoticed at its feet. Since that memorable first performance, poor Sister has hardly touched the keys.

In this tragical though expected and common *dénouement*—"poor Sister has scarcely touched the keys"—we have the clue to the disastrous effect, which we see all about us, of too much mechanical and professional music on musical taste. The loss of personal participation means the loss of the intimate sense of the soul of musical expression—melody. For this is substituted either some comparatively superficial interest, such as the curiosity of the habitual opera-goer or recital-enthusiast about personalities or mere brilliance of technique, or the purely sensuous enjoyment of the stimulus of crude rhythm of the "jazz-fan," or else complete indifference such as often alienates the plain man from music entirely. In other words, æsthetic sensibility, the love of beauty, which is the indispensable basis for love of the great classic music of the world, becomes paralysed or atrophied when there is no personal activity to sustain it. It may even never be awakened at all in childern who hear nothing but popular music produced by wholesale. In such unfortunates there will be either complete indifference to music, or at most a response to the crude nerve-stimulant of "jazz." Such people are the robots of a mechanized and dehumanised musical world.

Fortunately, however, music, like hope,

springs eternal in the human breast. The most complete scientific mechanisation, the most admirable modern organisation, cannot wholly discourage it. It sprouts as a weed in spring from under a steam roller. Thus Father, in Mr. Whiting's sketch, "discovers, after many trials, that the brazen readiness of the mechanical genius does not attract him; that while all the notes that Sister missed are sounded with authority, yet when he anxiously pushes the button marked 'expression' something is lacking which before gave him satisfaction. He longs to hear again the bashful, hesitating sounds which once charmed him, that human touch which said something to him, although imperfectly."

It is because the college glee clubs and orchestras have, consciously or unconsciously, made a discovery akin to Father's that they are so cheerfully singing and scraping and blowing, all over the country, at this moment. They hardly expect to rival the precision of intonation of a victrola record, the note-per-minute utterance of a pianola, or the beauty of tone and perfection of phrase of the Philadelphia Orchestra or the Flonzaley Quartet. But by actually struggling with a quartet by Haydn,

let us say, they are fitting themselves to appreciate it when they hear the Flonzaleys play it
far better than they could by buying any number of records of it. What is more, they are
bringing the plain man back to music, back from
indifference, and also back from jazz. They
are changing some of the dregs in the glass
into good beer. What they may eventually do
to the froth is another matter, and one of
fascinating interest, since the sterility of mere
professionalism is as evident in this day of
Schönberg, Scriabine, and Stravinsky, as the
crudity of the merely popular, and music obviously needs the plain man as sorely as he
needs music. The glee clubs and college orchestras and students in the settlements, then, deserve all the support we can give them; their
activities are of far more promise for our musical future than many that make much more
noise in a Babbitt-ridden world. If we spent
as many hundreds of dollars yearly on forming
ourselves into amateur groups to produce music
for the creative joy of it as we do thousands
on hiring professionals and manufacturing machines to amuse us, we should become a music-
enjoying and perhaps even a music-producing instead of a musically exploited people.

III

Should the amateur production of music be widely developed in the present movement for glee clubs and orchestras in colleges and schools, we should expect from it a deeply salutary effect not only on "low-browism," with its crude taste for "jazz" and ragtime, but also on "high-browism," from the affectation and sterility of which our contemporary music suffers quite as much. As the good beer increased in our musical glass, we should hope to see the froth as well as the dregs diminish. This would be the natural and inevitable result of bringing the emotional vitality of the plain man back into an art which for lack of it now too often hardens into professionalism or languishes into decadence.

If we look candidly about us at our professional music, we shall see the hallmarks of decadence on every hand. First of all, or at any rate more striking than any other symptom, is the almost universal preoccupation with manner at the expense of matter. A blasé intellectual curiosity about how music is made takes the place of the eager, child-like, æsthetic joy in music itself of the really creative periods.

40

When people become sophisticated they forget
the emotional object of expression, losing themselves in subtleties about its methods and materials, as the euphuists did in literature, for
example, and as our Schönbergs, Scriabines and
Stravinskys, and even to a large degree our
Debussys and Ravels, have done in music. Like
Schönberg they set themselves to devising a
super-counterpoint that flouts the limitations of
the human ear; or with Scriabine they invent a
"mystic chord" built on fourths, in defiance of
nature, or with the French "Group of Six"
they explore "polytonie" (several keys or to-
nalities at once), quite as the euphuists looked
up all the six-syllable words in the dictionary
or jumbled together all the similes in zoölogy.
They idolise what they call "originality," by
which they mean a search for oddity rather
than a masterly use of the familiar; [3] and they
prefer the uselessly complicated, cluttered up,
and messed about to the simple, the necessary,
and the noble, just as the euphuists would doubtless have preferred Cleveland's "innocuous
desuetude" to Lincoln's "With malice towards
none, with charity towards all," using as it does

[3] For a more detailed development of the contrast between
real originality and pseudo-originality, see "Artistic Ideals."

only words comparable to the standard harmonies of music: "triads," "sevenths" and "ninths," without any "elevenths," thirteenths," or "higher dissonances."

There is of course no reason why the most complex harmonies, the most ferocious dissonances, should not be used, provided the thought calls for them: it is the valuing of the medium above the thought that is decadent. Shakespeare, in his "The multitudinous seas incarnadine," is no euphuist. Monosyllables in this case would not have caught the flavor of his thought. Many phrases of Debussy, built on the far-famed "whole-tone scale," achieve a distinction obtainable in no other way; some of Stravinsky's dissonances are equally happy. But to all such matters two æsthetic principles apply, of which many modern composers seem either unaware or contemptuous. The first is that, since music is peculiarly an art of contrast, all its technical procedures depend for much of their effect on foiling against their opposites. The ear can, for instance, be easily habituated to any degree of dissonance, but for that very reason quickly loses the force of the dissonance unless the latter be carefully foiled against consonance. Progress here consists,

therefore, in widening the scope of the conso-
nance-dissonance antithesis, without ever losing
hold of its first term; so that to use nothing
but dissonance would obviously be, not very
bold, but only rather stupid. A Schumann can
make more effect with a mild *frottement* of
two tones than can an Ornstein by sitting on the
piano.

Good string-quartet writing, again, requires
infinitely delicate adjustments. To ignore the
basis of such adjustments is not the same thing
as successfully to solve each as it arises. One
can see what a lover of this beautiful and
almost obsolete art had in mind in replying to
an admirer of Schönberg, who had protested
that the viola part alone of his quartet was a
masterpiece: "Yes, the viola part alone is more
of a masterpiece than the whole quartet."
Similar considerations apply to "polytonie."
The older tonal system of Bach, Beethoven,
and Wagner is marvellously rich in its systems of relationship, its hierarchies of inter-
relationship, in and between keys—how rich
only the intelligent lover of classic music knows.
Unless the listener to two keys at once can hold
fast all these prior relations of at least one of
them (and it may be doubted if any human

mind could achieve such a feat) "polytonie" is in truth an impoverishment rather than an enrichment of the medium.

A second æsthetic principle even more important than any concerning the medium itself, however, is that all qualities of the medium are after all only means to ends, and these ends are the thoughts to be expressed. Now in music the thoughts are the melodies. It is the melodies that give its final character to a work of musical art; compared with them harmony is quite subordinate. Says M. Vincent d'Indy: "In order that harmony should be durable, it must constitute, not mere glistening surface, mere tapestry, but rather the clothing of the living and acting being which is the *rhythmed melody*. The costume, in this case, may safely pass out of style—the human person, if it is well constituted, will endure." Is it not obvious to any unprejudiced listener to most of the so-called "ultra-modern" composers that they have precisely reversed the normal condition, that much of their music is all harmony and no melody, all "glistening surface," tapestry, clothing, with no "living and acting being" beneath? Is not precisely this the reason why they are so uniformly dull—why they all sound so strangely

44

alike? It is only to the technically sophisticated that they seem bold revolutionaries; the only boldness of an artist is to have ideas; and however iconoclastic these men may be in harmony, harmony is secondary, and so far as they lack the imaginative force to project rhythms that shall seize the imagination of the listener, their final effect must be, to the plain man, and to the musician happy enough to retain some of the plain man's unspoiled simplicity, merely wearisome, flat and tame.

A technical analysis based on rhythm rather than harmony, on the essential, that is to say, rather than the superficial, would bear out the plain man's impression. It would tend to show that while "cerebrals" like Schönberg run to rather featureless, wandering rhythmic outlines, a group influenced by French impressionism and including such diverse personalities as Debussy, Ravel, Poulenc, Milhaud, Malipiero, Casella, Cyril Scott, and Goossens use, on the other hand, almost exclusively, short-breathed rhythms of a few notes, endlessly and monotonously repeated, often in combination with an ostinato or persistent figure.[4] Still another

[4] The quasi-mechanical repetitions of short phrases in Ravel's String Quartet, for example, beginning at the very

45

group, Prokofieff, Stravinsky, and Casella in part of his work, complete the downward curve of decadence and arrive back at the starting point of rhythmic development—the crude childishness of "jazz." Stravinsky's "Ragtime," Bela-Bartok's "Bear Dance," and even Debussy's "Golliwogg's Cake-Walk," are examples of how composers who might have advanced the great tradition of Bach and Beethoven can degenerate instead into second childhood, and take a noble art into the nursery to trifle with.

Thus in one way or another most of this music is as featureless in rhythm—the essential factor in musical originality—as it is futile in its more superficial harmonic complexities. Are its practitioners dimly aware of this ineptitude? Is it by a process of rationalisation that they so constantly, as theorists and apologists, erect into virtues their very defects as creators? Why do they so tirelessly tell us that melody is old-fashioned? Why have they tabooed as "banal" those composers who, like Elgar and

start, soon grow almost intolerable to a sensitive listener. Ernest Newman has commented on the "short breath" and in general the melodic insignificance of Ravel, truly pointing out that if you scratch his surface you find Chaminade underneath.

46

d'Indy, use themes, and as "academic" that
process of thematic development which can
never be denied to such themes, since "living
and acting beings" cannot choose but live and
act? Why do they insist always that music
must be entirely sensuous?—either agreeable
or disagreeable to the senses, preferably the
latter, but making no appeal to the æsthetic
imagination, the mind, or the spirit. Does it
not all look strangely as if they were the tailless
foxes of music?

Besides what d'Indy has called *"complications inutiles"* in harmony, besides poverty in
salient and broad-flung rhythmic design, such
as Clive Bell in another art has well named
"significant form," there is a third hall-mark
of decadence. This is a glorification of technical difficulty for itself, a worship of virtuosity, which seems to be the inevitable product
of professionalism in art. Though no doubt
partly commercial in origin, in one case as in
the other, it seems to develop also out of the
necessity felt in perfect good faith for masking
the fundamental emptiness of an art vacant of
human emotion by means of a portentous
elaboration of technique. Bach with an idea
can bring music out of a single violin; the mod-

ern who lacks it requires an orchestra of over a hundred men, and writes things for them that they can just barely play—and that we wish they couldn't. Not only has orchestral music become so difficult that only a few professional orchestras, after long and ever more expensive rehearsals, can play most of it, but piano and chamber music, those parts of the art where in all great periods it has touched the amateur most closely, are hedged off from him today by well-nigh impassable technical barriers. Imagine college pianists and violinists, instead of navigating, with some peril but endless delight, as we used to do, the varied and romantic seas of Grieg, Brahms, and Franck, venturing on the uncharted wastes and engulfing billows of Florent Schmitt! Fancy a string quartet of young business men regaling themselves in leisure hours with Stravinsky and Schönberg! There is no need for music to be so difficult, there is no sense or real skill in making it so. Such difficulty is rather a sign of impediments unremoved, of complications not thought through, of problems unsolved. If the young composer will but resolve to show his prowess, not by the crabbedness but by the ease of his product, he will at last have a task worthy of

48

his mettle. We may justly conclude that wherever difficulty becomes an end in itself the ideas it should serve are lacking. Nine-tenths of our modern music, in plain fact, is needlessly, injuriously, and stupidly complicated. Let us stop gaping at it in an equally stupid awe. Let us laugh it good-humoredly out of court.

In order to do that, however, we should have first of all to conquer in ourselves weaknesses akin to its own. We should have candidly to admit that we, too, were afraid to stand fearlessly and independently on our own æsthetic perceptions, that we were dominated by herd standards and conventions, that we were servile followers of prevailing fashions—in short, that we were snobs. And snobbism is always and everywhere the last and unfailing mark of decadence. If we wish to study in detail its characteristic mental processes, we have only to glance at any of the accepted organs of ultra-modernism, such as the *Dial* in America, the *Chesterian* in England, the *Revue Musicale* in France. In all of them we shall observe the same endless mutual admiration of the spokesmen of the "new" movements, the accepted vogues; the same panegyrics on each other's works, the same expositions of pet artistic fads; the same complacent ignorance or open contempt of all original minds which will not fall into their procession. In all we shall find the same curious use of question-begging epithets, such as "modern," "original," "radical," for those who "belong," and "old-fashioned," "academic," "pedantic," "conventional" for outsiders, without reference to such obvious facts as that no idiom could be more thoroughly conventional than that of French impressionism, for example, with its stock harmonies and its routine orchestral tricks—stopped horns, muted and divided strings, glissando harps, and the like. In short, we shall find on every page evidences of the exclusiveness described by Thoreau, by which we exclude ourselves from true enjoyments, and by which from time immemorial snobs have insulated themselves from the life-giving contact of plain men.

Thus it seems as if the most significant socio-musical phenomenon of our time, as will probably be recognised by future critics, is the segregation of several musical classes or castes (most strikingly that of the snobs) in inter-, national groups more or less disregarding national frontiers. Nationalism, however characteristic it may have been of the mid-nineteenth century, is far less so of the twentieth, though most critics, still dominated by nationalist conceptions, hardly realise the change. Nationalist, and even racial, distinctions have become comparatively negligible in modern music; they have been quietly replaced by class stratifications. The important division today seems to be that for which we have used the figure of a glass of beer, with its dregs, beer, and froth. Less figuratively, musical literature in our day seems to divide into three æsthetic layers or classes, to all of which the consideration of national origin is more or less irrelevant. First, there is the music patronised by the "low-brow," the music of dance-hall and street, for the most part as nameless as it is ephemeral. Secondly, there is the great music of all countries of the world, the music beloved of the plain man, whether it bear the name Bach, Beethoven, Mozart, Schumann, Schubert, Chopin, Wagner, Verdi, Tschaikowsky, Brahms, Franck, Elgar, Moussorgsky, or Strauss. Thirdly, there is music whose interest is less æsthetic than intellectual or social, which appeals to the curiosity and faddishness of "high-brows"; and here we find such varied names and incongruous juxtapositions as

Stravinsky, Scriabine, Schönberg, Ornstein, Malipiero, Casella, Satie, Milhaud, Griffes, Prokofieff, Goossens, Berners, and Bliss.

How totally irrelevant are national distinctions to lists made like these on the basis of a significant artistic contrast! What pertinent geographical comment could one make upon them? Is it not obvious that Prokofieff is far nearer to almost any other man in his list than to his compatriots Tschaikowsky and Moussorgsky, as they in their turn have more in common with any German, English or Italian composer in their list than with him? Shall we not group Goossens rather with Milhaud of Paris or Griffes of New York than with Elgar, Vaughan Williams, or Gustav Holst of London? Is Schönberg to be placed with his fellow-countrymen Brahms and Wagner, or rather with Casella, Malipiero or Stravinsky? No, modern decadence and its accompanying snobbism seem to be international, universal, and inescapable. Wherever music becomes over-intellectualised and is used as the plaything of a class, wherever it cuts itself off from the vitalising currents of human feeling, it dries up and withers away. On the other hand, and fortunately, the more healthy tendencies of our time seem to be as little confined within national frontiers as the less healthy ones. We easily forget that d'Indy is French, Elgar English, and Strauss German: we remember only that they all write good music. It is in an increase in the production and the appreciation of such international, universal music as theirs, made for no one nation, caste, group, or clique, that the hope of our future art of music must lie.

OUR ORCHESTRAS
AND OUR MONEY'S WORTH

WHEN Theodore Thomas started one
of the first orchestras in the United
States, his audiences received Wagner, then just
making his first difficult steps in Europe, with
some reluctance. "Why do you play Wagner
so much?" expostulated one of his players to
Thomas. "They don't like him." "Then,"
answered Thomas, "we must play him until they
do." Today our orchestras have increased in
number to about fifty, with twelve of major
importance, while in quality, thanks largely to
our wealth, they lead the world. Yet if they
are to fulfill their great promise, they still
need—in some ways need more than ever—the
leadership of men like Thomas. Are they to
give us genuine art, worthy of the traditions
we inherit from Europe and owe it to the
world to maintain to the full extent of our great
material power, or are they to be run on purely
business lines to supply the demands of the
majority, and is orchestral music to follow

among us the dismal path of the commercial
theatre?

Our answer will depend on the clearness of
our understanding of the conditions and nature
of artistic progress so strikingly implied in
Thomas's remark. Selling commodities for
profit is static, time-serving, and safe, a matter
of adjustment of supply with demand. Art is
dynamic, creative, experimental, innovating:
hence strenuous, venturesome, full of risk, succeeding only through failure, and demanding
alert activity of all who participate in it.
"Then we must play him until they do," implies,
first, Thomas's sense of the responsibility for
active leadership which has always animated
our greatest men, constantly rebuking but
never decisively conquering that opposite spirit
of commercial compromise with the crowd
which is the negative and uncreative aspect of
our American psychology. And secondly, it
implies something even more interesting. We
are to play Wagner, Thomas suggests, not
merely until people tolerate or endure him, but
until they like him:—and that is equivalent to
saying, until they understand him. Art is a
matter, then, in which not only we, but also
they, participate; it is strenuous and effortful

for them as well as for us; in short, it is conceived not aristocratically as the domination of
a passive herd by active masters, but democrat-
ically as the creative venture of all concerned.
This is a thoroughly modern conception of art
to which only the most alert-minded among us
are yet awake; it is something hoped for and
dimly visioned rather than fully achieved; and
inasmuch as the whole "appreciation of music"
movement is a reaching out towards it, it is
evidently as yet but very partially incorporated
in our actual musical life. It calls for an alert-
mindedness which, while thoroughly congenial
to the American temper at its best, is naturally
found only in the minority anywhere.

Thomas's remark thus affords a touchstone
for determining the vitality of our contemporary musical enterprises. To what degree is
their leadership far-sighted, adventurous, un-
compromising? To what degree is it calling
for the intelligent coöperation of that active-
minded minority of the public on the participation of which quite as really as on that of the
leaders, the vitality of the whole artistic process
depends? How successfully is it resisting the
temptation to compromise with the natural and
ineradicable inertia of the majority, for the

56

sake of ease, popularity, or financial return? If we apply these acid tests to our contemporary orchestras, what do we find?

I

In the matter of repertory, it may be suggested to begin with, we find too great a concession to the inertia of the majority which dictates that programs shall consist chiefly of the "safe and sane," the music that by the respectability of the names with which it is labelled saves us the trouble of discriminating its quality for ourselves. No doubt numerical preponderance in every audience must be conceded to the type we may call the moronic conservative. His psychology is interesting. The natural human indolence we all to some extent share with him determines his profound distaste for everything that demands effort, hence for everything new. He swears by the classics, not because he perceives their beauty (a highly active process) but because he recognises their names. He writes anonymous letters to composers still alive (in their music as well as in the flesh) upbraiding them for their "strange and ear-splitting sounds" and signed "A Lover of Music." This music that he burdens with his

57

love he regards not as a living and growing art, to which he might himself creatively contribute by understanding it, but as something long ago finished and conveniently classified, something kept on the shelves of libraries and exhibited in concert halls by famous conductors, quite as he regards what he calls "Art" and spells with a capital A, not as embodied in the houses, railroad cars, telephone booths, subway stations, and automobiles he lives among, but as preserved under glass or behind railings in museums. And this "museum music" of the moronic conservative thus becomes one of the ghosts, never laid, that mislead us from the pursuit of the real flesh-and-blood music that would make us happy.

Now of course undue concession to the taste, or lack of taste, of the moronic conservative, on the part of the leaders and policy-shapers of our orchestras, is a short-sighted and disastrous error. If you give people only what they are already familiar with, not familiarising them with anything new, you condemn them to a boredom which eventually boomerangs upon yourself when they decide to stay away from your concerts. There is something supinely servile and unenterprising in the attitude

58

of one of the best-known managers in New York, who openly asserts that symphonies popular enough with the large public to nourish the box-office are limited to a bare baker's dozen: Beethoven III, V, and VII, Tschaikowsky IV, V, and VI, Schubert's "Unfinished," Dvořák's "New World," César Franck, and all four Brahms. The constant repetition of these, with rival prima-donna conductors even playing the same one several times in the same month in the same hall, inevitably wearies the very public which had demanded them. And what is even worse, it denies it the familiarity with less popular works which would make it love them. Mr. B. H. Haggin in an interesting article on "Democracy and Music" [1] makes the specific charge that "the preferences of the majority are deferred to, and those symphonies are most played which will attract most money to the box office." "I do not deny," he continues, "that they are most of them genuinely great works—Beethoven's Fifth, for example, or the César Franck—analogous to accepted masterworks of painting that are on perpetual view in a museum. Nor do I, therefore, object to their being performed fre-

[1] *The Nation*, February 8, 1928.

quently; but I do object to other compositions being performed less frequently or not at all. What if certain acknowledged masterworks of painting had their faces turned to the walls of the museum and were allowed to be seen only once in five years, or two years, or one year? Yet that, in effect, is what happens to analogous masterworks of music." And of course it is not only the less-known works of great masters (such as Beethoven's Fourth and Pastoral Symphonies, Tschaikowsky's Suites, Schubert's C Major Symphony, Dvořák's Slavonic Rhapsodies, César Franck's *Variations Symphoniques,* Brahms's Tragic Overture) that are thus shelved; many lesser but delightful composers are elbowed out of the repertoire entirely.

Again, among standard works are comprised not only what we have called stand-bys, but what we may call "war-horses." These, as affording unequalled opportunities for personal display, are the especial favorites of guest and prima-donna conductors. They appeal to the inertia of the crowd in several ways. First, the works of Liszt, Strauss, Tschaikowsky, and Wagner, who may be taken as the chief purveyors of "war-horses," make their effects more through their dramatic or melodramatic qualities, through the sensuous richness, brilliance, and power of their orchestration, and through their use of programs or other literary means of inflaming the imaginations of the non-musical, than through the purely intellectual and emotional appeal of purer and greater music, such as that of Bach, Beethoven, Mozart, or Brahms. Hence they require far less concentrated attention, and are far easier to grasp up to a certain point, though never affording such profound delight. Second, being of a more external and sensational type of art, they lend themselves particularly to the posings, exaggerations, artificial and specious effects of the prima-donna conductor, and easily serve to set his personality in relief for those dull enough to prefer personality to beauty. They are thus well adapted to the low stage of mentality of those "fans" in every audience who conceive performers not as artists but as "stars," and devote themselves in the spirit of college athletics to "boosting" them. Did X make "Les Preludes" of Liszt more sensational than Y? ("Sensational" is a term of approval with such people, as with a certain type of commercial manager.) Did Y squeeze an extra

61

tear out of the finale of Tschaikowsky's "Pa-
thetique"? Did Z make the cellos drip more
honey than usual in Schubert's "Unfinished"?
And finally, laziness reaches its limit in those
who might be more properly called spectators
than audience, who indeed scarcely hear their
idols at all, so preoccupied are they in watching
them; and the Liszt-Strauss school is an admirable medium for pantomimic contortive conducting. How many of the fans could tell their
idol from the other fellow's, were both to con-
duct behind a screen? Let A make a perfect
balance of sonority, a beautifully gradual, even
crescendo, a dramatically just and expressive
pause, with that complete economy of motion
which is the ideal of art, and B bungle or caricature the same effect, but with a theatrically
striking gesture, and there is unfortunately little doubt which will receive the plaudits of the
crowd. Bruno Walter and Wilhelm Furtwängler, admirable artists, failed in New York
largely because they could not or would not cut
the necessary capers.

II

Taking now our five best-known orchestras,
the Philharmonic and the New York Sym-

phony,[2] the Boston, the Philadelphia, and the Chicago, let us set down for each, first, the percentage of "stand-bys" (Bach, Handel, Haydn, Mozart, Beethoven, Schubert, Schumann, Dvořák, Franck, Brahms) played in a single season, 1924-1925; second, the percentage of "warhorses" (Liszt, Strauss, Wagner, Tschaikowsky) played in the same year; third, the percentage of works by other standard composers played. Adding these together we shall get a line showing the total of standard works produced. Below this we may place the percentages of American works played during the same season, of other modern works, and the totals for modern works. If the figuring has been correctly done, the fourth and seventh rows (totals) should "prove" by adding up to just short of a hundred. These figures, of course, are not offered as having any binding scientific validity; for that they would have to cover all the major orchestras; and in any case such a merely quantitative summary would have to be qualitatively interpreted. But it is hoped that, if so interpreted, they may at least prove suggestive.

[2] These two New York orchestras have been merged into one since this essay was written.

FIGURE VI

TABLE SHOWING THE PERCENTAGES OF SEVERAL TYPES OF MUSIC PLAYED BY THE FIVE BEST-KNOWN ORCHESTRAS OF THE UNITED STATES DURING THE SEASON 1924-1925

	PHILHARMONIC Mengelberg, Von Hoogstraten, Hadley, Furtwängler, Stravinsky	NEW YORK SYMPHONY W. Damrosch B. Walter V. Golschmann	BOSTON Koussevitzky	PHILADELPHIA Stokowski	CHICAGO Stock
"Stand-bys"	34.11	33.33	23.14	26.66	25.6
"War-horses"	21.42	15.23	15.74	32.5	19.2
Other standard works	13.59	25.71	20.36	15.	20.8
Total standard works	69.12	74.27	59.24	74.16	65.6
American works	6.34	2.85	5.46	3.33	5.06
Other modern works	24.06	22.85	35.18	22.5	28.8
Total modern works	30.40	25.70	40.64	25.83	33.86
Total	99.52	99.97	99.88	99.99	99.46

The most striking thing in the first line of figures is the much higher percentage of "standbys" in the two metropolitan orchestras (34.11% and 33.33% respectively) than in the three orchestras serving publics more provincial, or at least less hectically urban. This is perhaps natural. The metropolitan orchestras are more subject to the commercial influences of rivalry between "stars"; they play to shifting audiences of transients and pleasure-seekers, out for sensation; they are peculiarly the victims of journalistic publicity-mongering. Can we divine a subtle connection here between the fondness of the Philharmonic management for displaying its "sold-out" sign and Sir George Grove's remark that "Beethoven's Fifth Symphony always fills the house"? Remembering, however, that the great classic composers, forming as they do the basis of all musical culture, ought to be heard every year, and that the mere fact that they are played is in any case far less significant than how they are played—whether as living beauty or as museum music for the morons,—we may do wisely to reserve judgment and pass on to the second line.

Here the most honorable record of least

65

. "war-horses" is held by one of the two metropolitan orchestras, the New York Symphony; and we cannot but reflect that Mr. Walter Damrosch, whatever his faults, is by no means a prima-donna conductor, while Mr. Stokowski and Mr. Mengelberg, whose war-horses bulk largest, have, in addition to their admirable qualities as musicians, great reputations as "stars" to be maintained. Unfortunately for them, moreover, the testimony of the third line, the very important one, artistically speaking, of less-known standard works given, strongly corroborates our impression that they are sacrificing a good deal to showmanship. Aside from the fourteen "best bets" of the stand-bys and war-horses, Philadelphia puts its money only on Berlioz, Bizet, Borodin, Bruckner, Chausson, Debussy, Gluck, Moussorgsky, Rimsky-Korsakoff, Saint-Saëns, and Weber, while the Philharmonic "also rans" extend only to. six of these, with the decidedly innocuous additions of Cherubini, Gade, and Mendelssohn. And it is precisely the metropolitan rival of this same Philharmonic that heads the list here—the New York Symphony under Mr. Walter Damrosch, whose fame as an interesting program-maker is thus afforded a statistical basis.

Qualitatively speaking, however, the most stim-
ulating and adventurous list of the lot is that
of Mr. Frederick Stock in Chicago: C. P. E.
Bach, Borodin, Bruch, Bruckner, Chabrier,
Cornelius, Glière, Goldmark, Humperdinck,
Moussorgsky, Rimsky-Korsakoff, Saint-Saëns,
Smetana, and Spohr. Few of the pictures in
his gallery are turned face to the wall.

III

We come now to modern works played, a
matter of crucial importance in view of our
principle that music is a living and growing art,
and that audiences have their indispensable
contribution to make to this life and growth.
What is a liberal policy with regard to modern
music? If it were possible to answer in purely
quantitative terms, we might simply take as a
model Mr. Koussevitzky's list in Boston, combining as it does the largest percentage of modern works (40.64) with the correlative smallest
percentage (59.24) of standard works. The
matter is, however, not quite so simple as that,
because of two qualitative considerations which
necessarily enter in: the representation given to
a class of works that occupy something the
same place in the modern repertory that stand-

bys and war-horses do in the standard, and the treatment allotted to American music.

To begin with, then, there is in every audience a type of person we may call the moronic radical. Less numerous as a class than his fellow conservative, he is far more vociferous, and unfortunately just as unintelligent. Both are the victims of mental inertia: the only difference is that the laziness of the one cares only for what is old, that of the other only for what is new. He demands the latest because he lacks the taste to recognise the best. His preference is for whatever is crudely eccentric, bizarre, ugly, and cynically sophisticated. He is ready to proclaim anyone a genius who will but write for percussion instruments only, or accompany his music with colored lights thrown on a screen, or strike the piano with his fists or forearms. Now it is evident that this sort of thing, the "freak" whose "modernity," so vociferously advertised by the self-appointed claque of the moronic radicals, is its only claim to an ephemeral journalistic interest, is of no greater importance to the real growth of musical art than the stand-by of the moronic conservative or the war-horse of the conductor-fan. And it is further evident that, so far as

prima-donna conductors desiring to pamper
their vanity or commercial managers bent on
publicity make concessions to what Frederick
Delius calls "attempts on the part of Russian
impresarios, Parisian decadents, and their
press agents, to degrade art to the level of a
side-show at a fair," they are substituting a
static commercial enterprise for a dynamic
artistic one, following a policy essentially illib-
eral, circumscribing and tending to stultify
healthy artistic life.

One cannot help wondering what an out-
spoken defender of the more permanent musical values like Delius would say to the fact that
the single modern composer most frequently
played by four of our five orchestras in 1924-
1925 was that *enfant terrible* of sensationalism, Stravinsky, with nine performances by the
Philharmonic, five in Boston, six in Philadelphia, and six in Chicago. Perhaps he would
only remind us that the composer was himself
appearing that year as a guest conductor, and
regard the statistics as throwing more light on
guest conductorship than on composition or the
progress of modern music. And he would
doubtless insist that, as for Mr. Koussevitzky,
his list of contemporary works was not only the

largest but one of the most interesting: Bax, Bliss, Fauré, d'Indy, Rachmaninoff, Ravel, Schmitt, and Stravinsky. The only other list that is even more many-sided is that of Chicago: Bartok, Bliss, Dale, Delius, Enesco, Fauré, Honegger, d'Indy, Rachmaninoff, Ravel, Sibelius, Stravinsky, and Vaughan Williams. This bears out the impression of catholicity of taste and wide artistic range we gather from Mr. Stock's selection of less familiar standard works. On the other hand, Philadelphia's list is both the smallest and the most freakish. Along with some more solid nourishment, it sprinkles a good deal of paprika in the way of Casella, Eickheim, Hindemith, Prokofieff, Varese, Ornstein, and Tailleferre. Taken together with the low percentage of less-known standard works and the high percentage of war-horses in the same column, this tends to confirm the impression of sensationalism in the program-making of the Philadelphia Orchestra.

IV

Of course the ugly duckling of our American concert halls is American music—and this in spite of our widespread pious hope that somehow we shall wake up some fine morning to find it turned by magic into a beautiful white swan. Its unpopularity is a fact to be realistically noted and understood, not one to be resented or denounced. It is natural and inevitable that more or less everybody should be against American music. Until recently even many of the composers themselves have been against it, through their lack of technical skill and experience, and their ill-judged attempts to compensate such lacks by "patriotic" propaganda and personal influence—the worst possible ways to help the growth of really vital native art. The public is against it, on the principle that no man is a prophet to his own people, and that the near and familiar lacks the prestige and picturesqueness of the foreign. As for the press and the box office, of course they follow the public—so far as they are able to understand it. Even the players in the orchestra are against it; commercial publication of orchestral music being highly problematic in America, they are usually obliged to decipher it with difficulty from manuscript parts full of errors.

With such an array of natural enemies, it is really surprising that *Musica Americana* is not extinct among us. That it is not only alive, but growing with some vigor, is due almost entirely to the vision and artistic enthusiasm of those of our conductors who are true artists. Considering that most of them are of foreign birth and therefore naturally in more complete sympathy with European music than with ours, and are the personal friends of many European composers, considering the thanklessness of their task in bringing American music before the American public and press, considering the ingratitude and carping criticism with which they are often rewarded even by the composers themselves, their devotion to our music is beyond praise. It will never be known how much American music owes to Mr. Frederick Stock alone, for example, who for years has given it his great skill and his tireless loyalty; and there are several others. Thanks to these men, we have today a living American music, which has been made the subject of a detailed study by Dr. Howard Hanson, director of the Eastman School of Music, in a paper originally read before a meeting of the Music Teachers' National Association, and afterwards printed in pamphlet form. It is interesting to supplement our meager percentage figures with Dr. Hanson's.

LIST OF AMERICAN WORKS PLAYED MOST
FREQUENTLY BY THE THIRTEEN LEADING
ORCHESTRAS IN AMERICA DURING THE
SEVEN SEASONS 1919-1920 TO 1925-1926.

CARPENTER. "Adventures in a Perambulator."
Concerto for Piano and Orchestra.

CHADWICK. "Anniversary Overture."

EICHHEIM. "Oriental Impressions."

GOLDMARK. "Negro Rhapsody."

GRIFFES. "The Pleasure Dome of Kubla Khan."
"The White Peacock."

HADLEY. "The Ocean."

HANSON. "Lux Æterna."
"Nordic Symphony."

HILL. "Stevensoniana."

MACDOWELL. "Woodland Sketches."
Second Piano Concerto.
"Indian Suite."

MASON.	Symphony in C Minor. "Russians" for Baritone and Orchestra. "Prelude and Fugue" for Piano and Orchestra.
POWELL.	*Rhapsodie Nègre.*
SCHELLING.	"The Victory Ball." "An Artist's Life," Fantastic Suite.
SKILTON.	"Indian Dances."
SOWERBY.	"King Estmere," Ballad for two Pianos and Orchestra. "Comes Autumn Time," Overture. "From the Northland," Suite. Piano Concerto.
TAYLOR.	"Through the Looking Glass," Suite.

NOTE BY DR. HANSON:

"These lists are based solely on statistics, and do not imply the superiority of the composers over other composers. The number of performances which these

74

works have received would indicate, however, that there is already a small orchestral literature which has found favor with the conductors of our orchestras." [3]

The conductor who is a true artist is thus the most loyal, as he is the most powerful, friend of our native creative musicians. But with the typical "prima-donna" or "guest" conductor, the case is sadly different. Consider, for instance, the following little international episode. A famous virtuoso of the baton, in charge of one of our wealthiest and most influential orchestras, was presenting a first performance of a difficult violin concerto by a greatly gifted American composer. On the same program was the popular "New World Symphony" of Dvořák. To it he gave so much rehearsal time that he did not even read over the concerto (which was of course in manuscript) until urged to do so, did not seriously rehearse it until the day before the concert, and even then learned it so slightly himself that when the concert arrived, he was obliged to draw out the intermission to undue length while he studied the score he was about to

[3] See "A Forward Look in American Composition" by Howard Hanson. Published by the Eastman School of Music, Rochester, N. Y.

75

"interpret." Asked by the composer why he had spent so much time on Dvořák's work, which the orchestra knew backwards, and so little on his own new one, he turned the tables with a neatness rivalled only by its naïveté. "Why," he replied, "everybody knows the Dvořák Symphony, I must play it just right. But nobody knows your concerto, so it doesn't matter how I play it."

Here we have a frank, not to say a shameless acknowledgment of the inevitable result of the guest conductor system, with its servile attempt to placate the public with familiar pabulum played by famous personalities, instead of leading it to sympathetically creative coöperation with what is new, experimental, and forward-looking in contemporary and especially in native art. Such an attitude is comprehensible perhaps in a foreigner whose chief relation to us is a financial one, but it is disheartening to find Mr. Walter Damrosch, in an article entitled "Listening Backwards" [4] thinking upside-down to the extent of suggesting that "the scarcity of great new music today is responsible perhaps more than anything else for the growing practice of importing guest

[4] *The Century*, November, 1927.

conductors." "Hearing the standard works played several times a season, year after year," Mr. Damrosch proceeds to explain, "the music public naturally asks to have its interest whetted, and the method many of our symphonic organisations use to satisfy this desire, is to put new personalities on the conductor's stand." It does not seem to occur to Mr. Damrosch that while the public's interest is being so agreeably "whetted" by the "new personalities on the conductor's stand," these same personalities are most effectually cold-shouldering any potential great new music that might be coming to birth among us.

New music, whatever its share of greatness, can only live and find itself in the concert hall, just as the statue is tested, so Emerson tells the young sculptor, by the light not of his studio but of the public square. And this life in the concert hall of the music not of dead foreigners but of living Americans—of this music that is just coming, here and now, to difficult and venturesome birth—requires not merely the physical fact of performance, but the psychical environment, the climate, the sunlight, so to speak, of active sympathy from the public—from their ears, from their hearts, from their minds. It

77

requires from them a more modern attitude than the stupid conservatism that fancies music to have been finished up, once for all, far away and long ago, or the equally stupid radicalism that is looking not for living beauty but for "thrills," oddities, or novelties. It requires, in fact, just that attitude of eager, intelligent curiosity that in the sister art of literature we have already, though only recently, achieved. We no longer suppose that literature was consummated by Greece and Rome, by France and Germany, even by the England of Thackeray and Dickens, or for that matter the New England of Emerson. An interest in Shaw, Barrie, and Galsworthy does not seem to us to excuse indifference to Dreiser, Anderson, Eugene O'Neill. In short, letters have come alive to us, largely because we have learned to share vividly, ourselves, in their life. But music is still moribund, or just stirring in its sleep. It remains to us either "classic" and dead, or, if contemporary, queer and remote; we respectfully study its manifestations in Italy, Germany, France, Russia—even England, which came musically of age a generation ago, but it never occurs to us that anything more worth listening to than factory whistles, motor horns, radio, and jazz could come out of New York, or Chicago, or Detroit, or Rochester; and we contentedly keep our concert halls museums instead of making them grow also into laboratories.

Is it not, however, rather unreasonable of us to expect our composers to produce an American music alone and unaided while we compel them to run the gauntlet of the moronic conservatives, radicals, and fans of the audience, the management with its eye on the box-office, the press with its nose for the exotic and its deep-rooted suspicion of the native, and above all the new personalities so profitably engaged in whetting our interest? Might we not somehow manage to divert a little of that interest to our own music, good, bad, and indifferent? Of course, most of it will be mediocre; but Heaven knows we listen to enough European mediocrities every season. If we are to have mediocrities, why not insist that they shall be as largely as possible American? Then we shall not be submitting to sheer futile boredom, slaves of fashion; we shall be doing something in its measure creative. We shall at the least of it be assisting in the elimination of the unfit, preparing the ground for the next harvest of great new music which, as all signs indicate, is quite as likely to grow up here as anywhere, if we will only give it a chance.

THE DEPRECIATION OF MUSIC

A MUSIC-PUBLISHING house not long ago issued a New Year's card assuring us, its patrons, that we are now living in "The Golden Age of Music." The card, purporting appropriately enough to be of gold, but in reality a clever imitation in gilt, went on to remind us that never before have so many people spent so much money on the art of Mozart, Beethoven, and Schubert. Another wealthy concern, manufacturing mechanical pianos, strikes in a catalogue *de luxe* the same clarion note. "We are living in an age of conquest. Life is daily becoming easier, safer, and more enjoyable to us through man's triumphs in myriad different fields. . . . Music—the greatest and most universally loved of the arts—has yielded to the genius of man. Its barriers have been broken down, its mysteries revealed, its hitherto hidden beauties unveiled." Resisting a temptation to substitute "deflowered" for "unveiled," we read on, our dazzled eyes seizing these high points: "Extension of symphony orchestras over America . . . buildings inadequate . . . enormous Hollywood Bowl of California . . .

great stadium of the College of the City of
New York . . . enormous endowments . . .
Eastman School at Rochester . . . Juilliard
Foundation in New York . . . Curtis Institute
in Philadelphia . . . administered to foster
talent for the Art" (fittingly spelled with a
capital A). But even so skilled a writer of
advertising copy cannot keep the vein all the
time. Presently, in one of those lapses from
commercial romance to mere truth that afflict
us all, he permits himself this anti-climax:
"These great opportunities have in themselves
created a growing desire not only to listen to
music for the pleasurable response that it
awakens in us, but also to understand what we
are listening to. . . ."—Millions invested, you
see, and in return a desire on the part of us
dear children the public not only for "pleasurable response," but actually to understand what
we are hearing!—It seems a paltry result for
an age so busily engaged in unveiling (or de-
flowering) music, a poor exchange for the age
in which Beethoven wrung a bare living from
the Viennese nobility while he was putting so
much new music into the world—yes, even with
the Hollywood Bowl, the Juilliard Foundation,
and the Curtis Institute thrown in. It looks

82

disturbingly like a Gilded rather than a Golden Age, an age seeking quantity for the sake of profit rather than quality for the sake of joy, in short, a mechanised age. If we want it to shake itself out of its lethargy, and do something new and worth while for music, it is high time for us, sternly putting away the pipe-dreams of business romance, to use a little of the realism of the artist, and soberly begin thinking out ways and means.

I

Our fundamental error seems to have been the too uncritical assumption that the methods of quantity production by machinery, with their conveniences of reduction of overhead, standardisation of product, ease of marketing, and the rest, which have so marvellously increased our material wealth, could be applied with equal success to our far more important spiritual interests, such as art. That is the tacit assumption of many contemporary *entrepreneurs*, interpreters, and propagators of art, and of even a good many of the artists themselves. It is supposed, because it is easier, quicker, more convenient, and more profitable to make shoes or ready-made suits by the million than by the

piece, that it is also more satisfactory to circu-
late songs, or sonnets, or sonatas, and perhaps
even to make them, in the same way. (The
modern popular song, for instance, is an example of a commodity made to specification, so
completely standardised that interchangeable
parts can be supplied on mail order.) We
have been slow to perceive that "art" by the
car-load, literature by the library, and music
from the machine are somehow vapid and taste-
less; that while all our feet are near enough
alike to wear the custom shoes without too
much pinching, and all our shoulders near
enough the same height to hang the ready-made
suits upon (with a little padding) our hearts
and minds are so very different that to adjust
art, and especially music, to all of them is only
to spoil it.

Take, for example, as a particularly obvious
illustration the case of radio. H. G. Wells has
told with his usual clairvoyance what must be
the experience of thousands of enthusiasts with
their now disused sets. "I quite understand,"
he says, "the stage of inauguration and the
eagerness and initial delight of a new toy. And
afterward there may be a kind of struggle to
keep on with the thing that began with so much

hope and has given so much trouble. But sooner or later boredom and disappointment with these poor torrents of insignificant sounds must ensue." Some of these insignificant sounds he particularises:—"Uncle Bray and Aunt Twaddle, usurping our hour with the children"—"tenth-rate music, played by the Little Winkle-Beach Pier Band" (Reader please supply American equivalent)—"Doctor Flatulent, being thoughtful and kindly in a non-sectarian way." Yet, he says, the initial hopes die hard. "There is still a craving for unsectarian religiosity, for faith in things in general combined with faith in nothing in particular. There is still a conception of some vast orchestra playing music to suit every mind and taste simultaneously." [1]

Wells here puts his finger on the fundamental and ineradicable defect of music from the machine: its standardised, wholesale, impersonal quality, violating the essential uniqueness, particularity, and personal reference of all vital artistic experience. We resent Uncle Bray and Aunt Twaddle not only for their platitudes, but because they are usurping *our* hour, they are

---

[1] "The Way the World is Going," by H. G. Wells, New York *Times Magazine*, April 3, 1927.

treating us as if we were "Everybody," we who know we are Somebody; and all music that tries "to suit every mind and taste simultaneously" is making the same fatal mistake. Commerce can appeal to everybody, but it is the essence of art that it has to appeal to somebody, and to somebody who can get something from it only if he reacts to it, meets it halfway, with his own responses and from his own point of view.

Compared with this apparently well-nigh insoluble psychological problem of the passivity of the listener, the mechanical problems of radio and other music machines, though serious, seem less difficult. As to those subtle and minute nuances of speed and of relative loudness both of successive and of simultaneous tones on which expressiveness depends, we are already far from that early model of the player which, as Mr. Arthur Whiting points out, "had the exuberant spirits of a machine-gun. The notes of Mendelssohn's Spring Song were shot out like bullets so that the musically-timid hastened to take cover." [2] Since those days

[2] "The Mechanical Player" by Arthur Whiting. *Yale Review*, July, 1919. Can Mr. Whiting suggest any escape for the musically-timid from the street-corner loud-speaker?

such remarkable progress has been made, in truth of both rhythmic and dynamic nuance, in such instruments as the orthophonic victrola, for example, that we should be cautious of dogmatic denial that something near perfection may be attainable here. At present the difficulty least satisfactorily met is the recording of differences in force of simultaneous tones. Once at a rehearsal of the Detroit Orchestra, Mr. Gabrilowitsch, making the cellos emphasise the "thirds" in all the chords, explained to an inquirer that strong thirds greatly enhance the richness of the sonority, as any listener can verify for himself, and that such prominence of the thirds was an avowed principle with Leschetizky in piano-playing. Certainly all great pianists use an infinite variety of internal stresses of this kind, which even today mechanical players can reproduce only in the most rough-and-ready, crude fashion.

Yet even if we make the large concession that, provided the subtlety of the problem were recognised in a scientific spirit by the manufacturers, virtual perfection might be achieved in recording any single given performance, a more fundamental difficulty remains. No true artist gives two successive performances of the same piece in exactly the same way. To do so would stultify his freshness. The only way he can embody in his performance the personally active, living element essential to all artistic experience—in listener and performer alike—is to play each time with the spontaneity of improvisation, to whatever degree the general treatment will no doubt remain the same. Here the living artist and the mechanical record obviously part company: the most fanatical manufacturer would hardly claim that his machine could improvise. Again, even so fundamental a matter as pace varies with the physical and nervous condition of the player. Mr. Adolfo Betti, leader of the Flonzaley Quartet, has made the interesting observation that tempos are always taken faster in the evening than in the morning,—doubtless a consequence of more alert nervous response. Everyone who has attended those pairs of concerts with the same program, given one in the afternoon, the other in the evening (like the Friday afternoons and Saturday evenings of the Boston Symphony Orchestra or the Chicago Orchestra, for instance) knows how much more electrical the atmosphere is, how much more responsive the audience, how much more exciting the music, at the evening performance. The difference is of course due to the nervous tone of audience as well as of players. Every performer knows that his performance really lives only when he is face to face with his audience. Every composer knows that it is only in living contact with its audience that he can judge his work.

Thus we are brought back again to the most difficult of all the problems of radio: how can any artistic experience have value, in which the audience is in a purely passive condition—in which it may turn off at any moment the performance, as an observer in a garage one Sunday morning saw a bored chauffeur turn off a religious service in the middle of a prayer, or, what is even worse, turn it on at any moment as a not quite successfully ignored background for conversation? Mr. Eric Blom, in a very fair-minded article on "The Influence of the Radio on Music in Great Britain," [3] in which he certainly does ample justice to the educational possibilities of broadcasting, seems tacitly to conclude that there is no remedy for this passivity of the listener-in. "One need not go to a concert of community singing," he insists,

[3] New York *Herald Tribune,* October 30, 1927.

"to see the public take part in a performance.
. . . By more subtle psychic currents does an
audience take its share in the rendering of any
work of art, for its mere presence, passive only
in appearance, inevitably reacts upon the performance." And his article ends by praising
the British Broadcasting Corporation for its
"broad-minded and disinterested recognition
that, wonderful invention though the radio undoubtedly is, it cannot replace direct contact
with the performer. . . .The ultimate triumph
of broadcasting over the habit of being present
at a performance would only mean that the
race of musicians is doomed to extinction from
spiritual laziness—which is, one may venture to
hope, absurd."

II

The tendency of the Gilded Age to manufacture mechanised music in quantity in order
profitably to sell it to a passive public is, however, unfortunately not confined to the so-called
mechanical instruments. The orchestra itself,
most glorious of all instruments, seems in some
ways to be undergoing a progressive mechanisation. For all their brilliance and luxury, our
orchestral concerts are obviously in many re-

spects unhealthy, artificial, even decadent, as may be realised by noting the hectic character of their life, the "showmanship" and constant advertising necessary to keep them going, the paucity of new music produced either here or abroad, and the sensational character of most of the new music that does reach performance. All these defects seem to be explicable in terms of the formula by which we have explained music from the machine: the exploiting of a passive public, for profit, through quantity production. It is true that the profit motive is far less obvious than in the case of commercial companies manufacturing mechanical instruments; one may even question how it can have any place in enterprises run, as all symphony orchestras are run, at a deficit. But it must be remembered that the reduction of a deficit may be as eagerly sought as the increase of a profit; that the millionaire who generously puts his hand in his pocket quite humanly likes to leave something there when he pulls it out again; and that as a plain matter of fact, the box-office, as everyone knows who has had anything to do with orchestras, is by no means a negligible element in the determination of their policies. In last analysis it is the box-office that dictates

quantity production, and that is therefore responsible for mechanisation of the product, loss
of quality, and degradation of public taste.

It is now widely admitted that all our major
orchestras give too many concerts. Here we
have a situation somewhat parallel to the dead-
ening routine introduced into the commercial
theater by the long-run system: the wearisome
repetition of the same work of "art" until the
art in it disappears in boredom, tired nerves,
and mechanical habit. The work required of a
conductor in the unduly shortened and over-
crowded concert season, with regular concerts,
children's concerts, popular concerts, concerts
on tour scheduled according to the time-table
and with little reference to human endurance, is
so taxing that few have the mere physical
strength for it, to say nothing of maintaining
what Emerson calls "frolic health" and considers necessary to artistic activity. No wonder rehearsal suffers; no wonder new scores are
eschewed by over-driven conductors; no wonder the classics, such at least as have no "war-
horse" possibilities, are often played without
rehearsal, and so perfunctorily as to strengthen
the natural feeling of the young that nothing
good was written before 1900; and no wonder

the art of interpreting a new work sympathetically and understandingly gives place to the
more necessary art of rehearsing a forty-min-
ute work in half an hour.

A study of the programs for a single season
of the five best-known orchestras in this country, the Philharmonic and New York Symphony, the Boston, the Philadelphia, and the
Chicago, recently showed unmistakably [4] a tendency on the part of all to feature the "stand-
bys" that are most acceptable to the lazily conservative members of the audience and the
"war-horses" eagerly welcomed by the sensation-seekers and the prima-donna-conductor
"fans," at the expense of the less-known standard works and of unsensational, especially
American, contemporary works. These are tendencies only too familiar to all thoughtful music-lovers, but it is interesting to compare their
manifestation in different orchestras, and to
meditate upon their causes. Observing, for instance, that the Philadelphia and the Philharmonic Orchestras stand lowest in percentages of
less-known standard works given, we may be
tempted to attribute it to the well-known prima-

[4] See the foregoing essay on "Our Orchestras and Our
Money's Worth."

donna tendencies of Messrs. Stokowski and Mengelberg; and if we notice further that their percentages of "war-horses" are also highest, our suspicions will tend to be corroborated. On the other hand, however, the fact that the two New York orchestras stand low, the Philharmonic in less-known classics and the New York Symphony in modern and especially in American works, inclines us to wonder whether their large floating metropolitan audiences of sensation-seekers, tending to regard conductors as "stars," concerts as matches between them, and audiences as partisans, do not put them at an artistic disadvantage with more provincial orchestras where there is less competition, less publicity, less journalism, and more music. Certainly one is inclined to think that the purest musical joy to be had in America today is in the concerts, delightfully free from empty virtuosity, of those provincial orchestras that happen to be fortunate enough to be in charge of really great conductors, such as the Boston, the Chicago, and the Detroit. This agrees with the statistical study, which places Boston and Chicago, all things considered, highest, as it places lower the two New York orchestras, and the near-New York Philadelphia.

94

Of course, again, the general tendency of sensationalism betrays itself not only in the works chosen for performance, but in the manner of performing them. Sensationalism is found wherever there is insistence on the dramatic, melodramatic, or theatrical side of music at the expense of its musical value, that is, its beauty; wherever there is exaggeration of contrasts both in tempo and in dynamics; fast played too fast, to take away our breath; slow pushed to sentimentality; loud made deafening; soft inaudible.[5] And wherever there is sensationalism, there is that vicious circle of influence between herd public and showman conductor that mechanises art into commerce. As a slavish wife makes a tyrannical husband, so a servile public develops captious virtuosi. The seemliness of our concert halls, so correctly soporific, so free from the clamor of comment, remarks, boos, and hissing of the European halls, is too often the cold respectability of artistic death. We do not even laugh at the humor in music. And now some of the more spoiled and dictatorial conductors are even denying us our one remaining activity of applause

[5] For further discussion of this aspect, see the essay on "Sensationalism and Indifference."

between the movements, our one muscular participation in the artistic experience, our psychological safety-valve. We shall become wholly correct and wholly lifeless, and ready, leaving the concert halls become intolerable, to embalm ourselves in the living death of radio.

III

What, then, is to be done about it all? The practical thing would seem to be, recognising the degeneration inevitable to all art made in quantity, to reshape our musical aims and methods, consciously to abjure quantity and seek quality, and to arrange matters so that commercial profit is not necessary to the success of our undertakings. Those wealthy men who now support our orchestras at an annual deficit, at least those of them who do it for love of music and not for social prestige, might be willing to accept a larger deficit if they recognised it as the only means of resisting the degradation of the box-office. In the case of those orchestras that are supported by the subscriptions of many less wealthy persons, wide understanding of the conditions here described will be necessary to insure wise policies. Fortunately, we have before us the object lesson of the theater, where commercialism and professionalism have gone hand in hand to degrade, and where in recent years the amateur spirit, as expressed in the little theater movement, has begun to renovate and upbuild. Our metropolitan concerts have become almost as commercialised and professionalised as our Broadway theater. What we need is to develop the saving amateur spirit, not only in the concert hall, but in the college and school orchestra, the glee club, the singing society, the chamber music group—everywhere that it is possible to make music humanly rather than mechanically.

More broadly, we need to revise some of our ideas about popular education, and especially about the relation of the masses to the arts. "Leave this hypocritical prating about the masses," wrote Emerson many years ago. "Masses are rude, lame, unmade, pernicious in their demands and influence, and need not to be flattered, but to be schooled. I wish not to concede anything to them, but to tame, drill, divide, and break them up, and draw individuals out of them. . . . Masses! The calamity is the masses." Yet we have never learned the lesson; indeed, we have gone on flattering the masses more and more (under the pretence of schooling them) until our age, at best one of unprecedented popularisation, has become at worst one of unashamed vulgarisation. The motive has been fine. Emerson himself says in the same essay: "Nothing is so indicative of deepest culture as a tender consideration of the ignorant." Sir Hubert Parry, one of the noblest of modern musicians, fully recognised, as he shows in the chapter on the "Influence of Audiences" in his "Style in Musical Art," the menace of the uglier side of our public, what his biographer calls "raucous self-assertion, obscene gestures, contempt for lovely things and noble creations of art, and the desire to abolish them." Yet, the biographer adds, he "excused this attitude. The offenders never had the chance to understand this beauty. They knew no better; the fault was not theirs; they had been trodden down, and signalise their emancipation by an orgy of earthly pleasures and crude excitements." And Parry's conclusion was: "The mind that has the widest range tries to see into the mind that has the least."

But the fine effort of our humanitarian age to love the sinner has too often misled us into loving the sin too, or at least not hating it with clearness and enthusiasm. "Universal education"—so used to exclaim a clear thinker with a picturesque vocabulary, "is the trotting out of a damn' fine thing to a pack of idiots." Has is not too often been so? Has not "music for the masses," in particular, proved at best a delusion, at worst a prostitution? Is it really useful to anyone to put inane words like "Goin' Home" to Dvořák's beautiful Largo in the "New World Symphony," or to "jazz up" the Chopin Fantasie-Impromptu and call it "I'm Always Chasing Rainbows"? The other day one of the richest companies for manufacturing mechanical music in New York offered $20,000 in prizes for the completion of Schubert's "Unfinished Symphony." Some recalcitrant critics objecting that this showed ignorance rather than appreciation of the uniqueness of Schubert's style, and that one might as well add arms to the Venus of Milo, a man-to-man canvass was taken of the opinions on these artistic questions of the passers-by on Forty-second Street. One man gave an answer as brief as it was breezy. He thought that both the symphony and the statue should be finished—two movements for Schubert, and two arms for the Venus. What an admirable and truly democratic simplicity! Yet for one who might be thought to listen

99

closely and to good purpose to the voice of the people, Henry Ford, it is far from being the voice of God. "The old car was too slow," he told an interviewer. "The public was satisfied with it. And that's a sign we ought to change to something better. Since the public does not tell us what it wants, we give it what it ought to have." If that is true of cars, how much more of music! Bach acted on Ford's principle. He did not wait for the man in the street to like his fugues, and we need to learn that they can get along very well without each other. After all, in the nature of things, the appreciation of music can be only for the intelligent; all that the participation of the unintelligent is likely to bring about is the depreciation of music. Why not stop leading unthirsty horses to the water? They only muddy it.

SENSATIONALISM
AND INDIFFERENCE

THE boy who cried "Wolf!" was a poor
psychologist, because he forgot that a
stimulus repeated too often, or without reason, loses its appeal. Many of our modern
musicians, making the same error, are sur-
prised when their sensationalism breeds in the
public not interest but indifference. They do
not realise how quickly our bodies grow cal-
lous to even the keenest sensations, and how
necessary it is for anyone who would enlist
our permanent interest to appeal not only to
our senses but also to our hearts and minds. A
wider realisation of this simple psychological
fact would have far-reaching practical effects.
It is hardly too much to say that it would transform many of the activities of both our composers and our performers.

For over a generation now composers have
been chiefly preoccupied with harmony and harmonic effects, that is to say with the moment-
to-moment appeal of music to the senses, rather

than with the more synthetic appeals, appre-
hended by the mind, of melody and rhythm.
The kinds of momentary effect they specialised
in of course varied widely: the point in common
was the concentration on the sensuous moment
rather than on the mental span. Debussy and
his fellow Impressionists or Symbolists, for instance, sought an impalpable, evanescent, vague
harmonic coloring, richly caressing to the sense,
but comparatively empty for the mind through
the triviality of the melodic and rhythmic features, and thus discouraging all definite response
in us, inviting us to surrender ourselves to our
day-dreams.[1] Their followers the Primitives,
headed by Stravinsky, carried the same process
farther. They abolished the slight mental appeal that still remained in impressionism by re-
ducing melodies to short patterns of a few
notes, and rhythms to mechanical formulæ
monotonously repeated. At the same time they
greatly intensified the sense appeal of the harmony by making many more notes sound at a
time, many of them often ferociously dissonant.
They thus pushed the sense element to the
greatest luxury available to modern science at

[1] See the essay on Debussy in the present writer's "Contemporary Composers."

the same time that the mental element was reverting virtually to savagery.

Now the curious result was that this steadily increasing concentration on physical stimuli defeated itself, and instead of permanently increasing our excitement only keyed us up for a while, and when the novelty wore off left us jaded and bored. Indeed the very craving for that kind of excitement was a symptom of a morbid artistic condition, and just as the exhausted man finds himself only more exhausted after the brief fillip of a stimulant has passed, so the kind of listeners who were bored before Debussy mixed for them his draught of "dominant ninth chords" and whole-tone scales, having now followed his perfumed julep with Stravinsky's hard liquor have lost taste for either and find themselves more bored than ever. The ear quickly accustoms itself to any combination of sounds whatever, so that however eager aural curiosity may seem at any moment, as when Goossens, Milhaud, or Casella write in several keys at once or Mr. Henry Cowell plays the piano with his whole forearm, satiety is always just round the corner. Therefore the poor stale smell of Stravinsky's biggest and boldest tonal firecrackers, once they are exploded, might have been anticipated long ago by any lover of real musical values. Indeed it was anticipated by implication in a memorable remark made by Jean de Reszke in the early days of the Debussy *furore.* "Debussy is all right," said Mr. de Reszke, "for bored people, *but I am not bored."* Music lovers who use their minds and hearts as well as their senses seldom are.

For the interpreter no less than the composer indifference seems to be the unexpected but inevitable result of sensationalism. The generalisation throws light on many practical questions: on the paradox of guest conductors, for instance —why it is that the public demands so many new personalities, yet so quickly tires of them all. The "prima-donna conductor" is the victim of his own sensationalism; the "hit" he makes is brief in proportion to its violence, and the hero of today is neglected and contemned tomorrow. This is in last analysis because "effects" and "interpretations" deal with moments as brief and as detached from their context as the isolated chords of the mere harmonist, and the pursuit of them disrupts higher beauties just as harmony-worship distracts from rhythm and melody. Consequently in both cases contempt

follows on the heels of familiarity. The conductor often begins innocently enough by emphasising some special feature of the music,
on which the public at once seizes as the mark
of his "personality." Soon it proves to be
beyond human nature, in its pursuit of the "individual reading," not to push emphasis to overemphasis, overemphasis to distortion, and distortion to caricature. The whole, in which alone
is beauty, has disappeared in the sensations of
the parts, and the public, without knowing why,
has lost interest.

Take for instance the matter of dynamic
shading. Every artist knows that loud and soft
are not absolute but relative values.[2] Conductors, however, playing as they do in large
halls and for inattentive listeners, are under a
great temptation to abuse the loud end of the
scale. Especially a vigorous, full-blooded temperament like that of Mengelberg, admirable
musician though he be, is easily beguiled into too
energetic an assertiveness, and is apt in such
pieces as Liszt's, where much sound and fury
often signify little or nothing, to use, as the
English say, a Nasmyth steam hammer to kill
a fly. Even the more distinguished sensitiveness

[2] For examples see "The Tyranny of the Bar-line."

of a Stokowski cannot always resist his brass and percussion departments. Stokowski's immensely impressive orchestral transcription of Bach's great organ passacaglia became *too* impressive at its brassy end. Its body, so to speak, outgrew its mind. "A great master like Bach," observes Parry, "is instinctively aware that appeals to sensation must be accompanied by proportionate appeals to higher faculties. . . . The glory of Bach's management of such things is that the intrinsic interest of the music itself is always in proportion to the power and volume of the actual sound." But not even Bach's thought was quite in proportion to the overwhelming sound of Stokowski's trumpets and trombones; and with the loss of regard for limitations came a loss of artistic proportion and the dignity of restraint.

Pianissimos as well as fortissimos may be exaggerated. The "breathless pianissimo" is a pet device of the sensation-monger, a device which becomes inartistic the moment it focusses upon itself, a detail, the attention which should be spread over the whole scale of values. That is what sensationalism always is: disproportion, lack of proper subordination, the usurping by details of the place to which only the whole—

which is beauty—is entitled. Such a mere ghost
of tone, which one has to harken to painfully,
with suspended breath, to hear at all, as Koussevitzky makes in Schubert's "Unfinished Symphony," is almost as much out of the picture as
those apoplectic vehemences of Mengelberg. It
is too soft, as those are too loud; and to be too
much anything is the fundamental negation of
art, which is right order and proportion. A
subtle principle of style, moreover, is involved
here. What is too soft for Schubert might well
be exactly right for Debussy. There are various styles, and a value that fits one may not fit
another. One of the fundamental qualifications of the truly great conductor, which we find
preëminently in men like Stock, Gabrilowitsch,
Bruno Walter, and Furtwängler, is an unerring
sense of fitness of style.

Exaggerations of pace disrupt unity no less
than those of force, and are if anything even
more common. It is not a question so much
of taking certain entire pieces too slow (Wagner's Prelude to "Tristan" is a peculiar victim
of this tendency) or others too fast (such as
Smetana's "Bartered Bride" Overture, which
many conductors take at breakneck speed in order to exhibit their orchestras' virtuosity) as of

due proportion and relation between the parts of a single piece. We all know conductors who never play the lyrical second theme of a symphony in a pace bearing recognisable relation to that of the more energetic opening theme. This habit of automatically slowing up as if the "song theme" were a traffic sign is peculiarly annoying. It breaks fatally the continuity of the movement, and turns it into a series of pieces. Some conductors are seduced into it by a desire to underline the "expressiveness" of the song theme, not realising that sentimentality is never so moving as sentiment; others take the more vigorous parts so fast in the interest of orchestral brilliance that the pace, when the expression changes, is obliged either to moderate or to become palpably absurd. But whatever the motive for this disruption of continuity, the interesting point to note is that it is invariably punished, as all such disruptions are, by loss of interest. For every such transgression the law of beauty—wholeness, balance, proportion—is automatically and instantly avenged. You can make your momentary effect, but your larger and more persuasive appeal, the atmosphere in which your whole work reposes, is thereby dissipated and annulled.

Hence the singular dullness of all forms of overemphasis in art. . . . Mr. Olin Downess [3] tells a delightful story of "Toscanini's Scale." The orchestra was practicing a Beethoven symphony which it had often played under another conductor. This conductor had liberally marked up the players' parts. Suddenly an innocent scale passage was played with a terrific and portentous crescendo. Mr. Toscanini stopped and demanded the reason. "It's marked in our parts." "Rub out the marks," he said. "Beethoven has written a scale there, and nothing else. Please play me, without any expression, a scale—simply a scale."

There are certain kinds of overemphasis that under modern conditions seem well-nigh inescapable, even by conductors of the most sensitive taste. Too much and frequent accent, by players demoralised by moving picture house and dance hall orchestra service makes it almost impossible to play a delicate classic like Mozart as he should be heard. Here the details are the single accented notes, and the beautiful whole they destroy is the long, quiet, level Mozartean phrase that must float like a cloud,

[3] In the New York *Times,* January 29, 1928.

as it were, in a windless air. Modern players tear these phrases into shreds. Stokowski once spent ten minutes of a rehearsal making his first violins, playing alone, repeat many times a single phrase toward the end of the slow movement of Mozart's "Jupiter Symphony." He was trying, as you might say, to take the "kinks" out of it, to smoothen and extend it, until, accentless or nearly so, it should take on the perfect serenity and repose of classic beauty. A thankless task, one might say. Certainly a difficult one, since we live in a noisy and distracted age where few have the patience to achieve beauty, and few the repose to appreciate it. But not thankless; for since beauty is the only lasting value in art, those who have not been led through sensationalism to disillusion and indifference are constantly reawakening, often when they least expect it, to the joy in which alone is permanence.

STRAVINSKY AS A SYMPTOM

I

THE proverbial small boy's idea of "poetry" is a relentless recurrence of two-syllable groups, all exactly alike:

> The *boy* stood *on* the *burn*ing *deck*
> Whence *all* but *he* had *fled*.

If the Juggernaut march of accents happens to bring a stress on an unimportant word like *on*, so much the worse for the sense. As he grows up, however, if his feeling for rhythm develops, he may come first to perceive, then to tolerate, finally to relish verses of less mechanical inflexibility, in which vital displacements of accent are effected by important words. He may come to savor such subtle groupings as these of Masefield:

> I must go down to the sea again, to the lonely sea and
>   the sky,
> And all I ask is a tall ship and a star to steer her by;
> And the wheel's kick, and the wind's song and the
>   white sail's shaking,

And a grey mist on the sea's face, and a grey dawn
breaking.

Even the greatest poets and composers often
go through essentially the same development.
Wagner, as Ernest Newman has pointed out,
began with the small boy taste for sing-song,
and many of his early tunes are as angular and
monotonous as, for example, the march in
"Tannhäuser." Only gradually did he feel his
way to the beautiful elasticity of the Spring
Song in "Die Walküre" and the Good Friday
Spell in "Parsifal." It took Verdi the better
part of a lifetime to pass from the crudity of
"Trovatore" to the freedom of "Falstaff" and
"Otello." What the psychologists call our
spans of apperception differ not so greatly, perhaps, in absolute measurement, between the
rawest and the most cultivated mind; but the
variation, however limited in quantity, is qualitatively immensely significant; it is what chiefly
distinguishes the lover of Beethoven or Brahms
from the child or the savage still in the tom-
tom stage.

That the majority of what we are pleased to
call our musical public are still in this childish
or savage stage of taste is shown by the popu-

larity of jazz. Jazz is the doggerel of music. It is the sing-song that the schoolboy repeats mechanically before he becomes sensitive to refined cadence. It is not, accurately speaking, rhythm at all, but only meter, a monotonous repetition of short stereotyped figures. For precisely this reason is it popular with listless, inattentive, easily distracted people, incapable of the effort required to grasp the more complex symmetries of real music. If I am so dull that I cannot recognise a rhythm unless it kicks me in the solar plexus at every other beat my favorite music will be jazz, just as my favorite poetry will be "The boy stood on the burning deck" or its equivalent. If I possess, moreover, the conceit of the dull, I can easily go on to rationalise my preference into a canon of universal excellence, and affirm that jazz is the only music for all true Americans. And if I have also the hostility of the dull to all distinction, the desire to pull everything above me down to my own dead level of mediocrity that seems to be a part of our American gregariousness, I can complete my æsthetics by "jazzing up" whatever genuine music may happen to come in my way. With Paul Whiteman I can render Chopin indistinguishable from Gersh-

win, I can reduce Beethoven to terms of Irving
Berlin, and, like some perverse tonal Burbank,
I can transform MacDowell's "Wild Rose"
into a red cabbage.

Of course, the propagandists of jazz are always assuring us that there is in it a new
rhythm, the famous ragtime snap or jerk. Our
answer must be that this novelty, such as it is,
is not rhythmical, is hardly even metrical, is in
fact but superficial, as if our schoolboy should
whistle or squeak before each word of his dron-
ing line. Fundamentally, jazz is an insufferably
mechanical two-beat time, with a whack on the
big drum for every down beat. To condemn a
lover of music to sit through a concert of such
stuff is to closet Shelley with the schoolboy for
a whole evening. So arid is the sameness that
even a three-beat measure of common waltz
time refreshes like a spring in a desert. There
are people who seem to think there is something shocking about jazz. Ah, if there only
were! It is its blank featurelessness, its unrelieved tepidity, that are so pitiless. Like all
primitive forms of art it is so poverty-stricken
in interest for the mind (whatever its luxury
of appeal to the senses through mere mass of
noise or through odd effects of muted trumpets,

squeaking clarinets, or flatulent trombones),
that it kills its victims by sheer boredom.

Now, if we were to take this formula of jazz
—short rhythmic or metrical figures, formally
inane but physically pungent, mechanically repeated—and put at its disposal all the resources
of modern musical technic, particularly in the
matter of complex harmony and tone-color,
what should we get? We should get, should we
not, the so-called ultra-modernist composers,
headed by Stravinsky? . . . The reason we
do not usually recognise this curious æsthetic
kinship, this atavism by which the traits of savage ancestors reappear in neurotic descendants,
is that the modernist composers have drawn
the red herring of harmony and tone-color
across their trail. A page of Stravinsky is so
much more sophisticated in technic than a page
of Gershwin that we do not realise that æsthetically they are tweedledum and tweedledee.
But harmony and tone-color are matters of
superficies, not of substance. Take a banal bit
of melody, and reduplicate it at as many levels
as you please, as in the favorite "parallel dominant ninth" chords of Debussy or the more
ferocious dissonant combinations of Stravinsky,
and though you lavish upon it all the exotic

colors of your jazz band or Stravinskian orchestral palette, it can never become anything but
the banal melody it was at first. Harmony and
color are only costume; the persons of music
are the rhythmed melodies; and dress them as
you will they remain fatally themselves, like
the tramp in the story who awoke in the king's
palace.

Well, the Stravinskian melodies are just the
jazz tunes over again, more strangely and
handsomely dressed. They are the tramp in
the king's crown and robes. No doubt the
crown is dazzling bright, the robes of irides-
cent silks and luxurious brocades: Stravinsky is
a master of the orchestra. But he is no master
of rhythm—rather the slave of metrical formulæ. Of the final dance in the *Sacre du Prin-
temps* Cecil Gray remarks in his "A Survey of
Contemporary Music":

The time-signature changes constantly from bar to
bar, but the music itself does not. There is nothing
there but the incessant reiteration of the same insignificant metrical phrase in slightly varying quantities.
. . . Rhythm implies life, some kind of movement or
progression at least, but this music . . . is like a top
or gyroscope turning ceaselessly and ineffectually on
itself, without moving an inch in any direction, until,

in the last bars, it suddenly falls over on its side with a lurch, and stops dead.

It is this piecemeal, mechanical, inorganic structure that seems, despite other differences, to be characteristic of the whole contemporary movement of which Stravinsky is the outstanding figure, and even of the earlier impressionism from which it derives, partly by continuation and partly by reaction. Modern music avoids long living curves of rhythm, and becomes ever more choppy and more mechanical. In Casella and Malipiero, in Ornstein and Prokofieff, in the French Group of Six, even in Debussy and Ravel we note the same reliance on brief bits and snippets of tune, on stereotyped *clichés,* and on the *ostinato,* that degenerate modern grandchild of the savage tom-tom. It is a decrepit, senescent, decadent art that we see all about us, slowly dying of hardening of the arteries.

II

To what extent is this second childhood of our music to be attributed to the influence of the general public? Does the public really like that sort of thing? And if it does, is there much chance of our ever getting anything better? A statistical investigation of the taste of a large section of that public in the sister art of poetry, undertaken by Professors Allan Abbott and M. R. Trabue,[1] certainly seems to show a crudity of perception, a preference for obvious and rigid over subtle and vital rhythm, alarmingly widespread. Messrs. Abbott and Trabue reduced to jingle the Masefield stanza given above by replacing its elastic rhythms with mechanically regular anapests, thus:

I want to get down to the ocean again, to the wonder-
    ful sea and the sky,
And all that I ask is a ship of my own and a compass
    to steer her by,
And the pull of the wheel and the sound of the wind
    and the glistening rigging so free,
And the grey of the dawn coming up o'er the bow,
    and a mist on the face of the sea.

Of thirty-five hundred students asked to choose between this sorry sing-song and the original, a majority in grades, high school, and college actually preferred the sing-song. It was

[1] "A Measure of Ability to Judge Poetry," published by Teachers College, Columbia University. See also "Pegasus in the Paddock," by Winthrop D. Lane, the *New Republic,* January 7, 1925.

only graduate students whose taste was mature and individual enough to pick out the more beautiful form. It seems that the perception of an elastic beauty requires a more sustained power of attention than most people have, and that they find the path of least resistance in "setting" their responses to short spans like unvarying anapests and letting them grind away automatically. "Disturbance of the rhythm," write Messrs. Abbott and Trabue, "spoils poetry for most readers; and they count it disturbance to introduce inversion of accent, unexpected pauses, and other subtleties."

Can we doubt that most listeners to music are in rhythmic feeling equally childish? As we look about a concert hall at the faces of the audience, so little concentrated, so easily distracted, so incapable apparently of sequacious thought or feeling, can we wonder at the popularity of the most banal and obvious sing-song in the "hits" of the day in musical comedy, rag-time, and jazz, at the eager response, on a somewhat higher plane, to primitives like Stravinsky and decadents like Debussy, at the long indifference to anything more subtle or powerful, making it take decades for Brahms to get the ear of the general public, if indeed he ever gets it? We have all read how Beethoven slowly and laboriously created the lovely theme of the Andante of his Fifth Symphony from an unpromising germinal form found in his sketch-book, crude in balance as a street song. When we sit in Carnegie Hall waiting for the concert to begin we cannot help wondering whether most of the audience would not really rather hear the sketch than the perfect melody.

Perhaps they would, at any one concert. Yet the element of time must work for the finer thing, obviousness must grow stale in the long run, and quality tell. Condemn the dullest to read daily both versions of the Masefield stanza, and one would say that at the end of a month either the spoiled version would have driven him mad or the contrast of the beauty of the original would have won him to sanity. Beethoven's Fifth Symphony would be unendurable by now if he had been satisfied with his sketch. One could make a very pretty fantastic theory that the higher and subtler qualities to be noted in any piece of art at any time are not the causes of its success in the immediate sense of being appreciated and acclaimed by this public now, but are only responsible, so far as the great public is concerned, for its survival over other things that have become too threadbare to be longer endured. We cannot stand Meyerbeer any longer, though his contemporaries preferred him to Wagner; nor Spohr, though he was ranked above Beethoven in their lifetimes; nor Mendelssohn, so much the popular hero when Schumann was still ignored. In the same way we may suspect that our descendants will find the monotony of Stravinsky's primitive rhythms intolerable. Indeed, some of his contemporaries are beginning to find them so already. Boredom, for the popular idol, is the beginning of the end. And so Stravinsky may turn out, after all, to have been the superman, not of music but only of jazz.

TWO CRITICS OF
ULTRA-MODERNISM

DR. GEORGE DYSON, in his "The New
Music," and Mr. Cecil Gray, in his "A
Survey of Contemporary Music," have given us
together something like a complete analysis of
the characteristic viewpoint, aims, and methods
of ultra-modernism. Dr. Dyson, accepting the
interest in momentary harmonic combinations
as the characteristic musical interest of our
period, devotes almost half his space to a systematic and interesting analysis of "texture."
Pointing out that the last great period when
texture occupied this paramount place was that
of Bach, and that "modernity in this sense has
synchronised with a growing appreciation of
Bach," he begins by contrasting the two types of
texture. "The normal texture of Bach is contra-
puntal. . . . Modern texture is normally vertical, harmonic, a fabric of splashes of sound.
. . . Our values are at right angles to those of
Bach. We exploit masses and contrasts, and
the medium is color rather than line; the fabric
is wall-paper rather than tapestry." He imag-

ines Bach examining the music which came after him and which, in Beethoven's tonal architecture as in Haydn's and Mozart's neat lyricism, turned away from his ideals. "Finally, he would reach our humble selves. What have we to show him? The pretty tunes are foresworn, the architecture is melting, the external dramas and labelled themes are a little out of fashion. One or two minor developments are new, at least in degree; in particular, the wealth of local colors and of semi-barbaric rhythms. Asia and Africa are imported into the concert-room, and the drum is beaten harder than ever before. . . . There remains of our inheritance a predominantly vertical texture, an ever-increasing apparatus of sound, and a consequent leaning towards harmonies and rhythms which are new, or rich, or strange."

The originality of Dr. Dyson's book lies chiefly in the ingenuity with which he traces the development of ultra-modern texture from traditional harmony by wholly natural and inevitable extensions of usage. No former book, not even that of Lenormand or that of Dr. Eaglefield Hull, has succeeded so well in showing the *rationale* of ultra-modernism. Conceptions such as that of the complication of traditional chords by added appoggiaturas and passing-notes and by the "elision of implied resolutions" are exceedingly illuminating. Many valuable critical *obiter dicta* are generated from them. For example: "The formal element in Scriabine's harmonic system is his use of a chord of classical derivation, made more complex by added appoggiaturas, and elevated into a kind of anagram of a whole movement. It is this that makes so much of his music, once the novelty or the color of it has worn off, harmonically monotonous." For Debussy's pet process of moving a whole harmonic mass as if it were a single melody Dr. Dyson invents a name that deserves to pass into general parlance; he calls it a "side-slip." And he acutely remarks: "The logic of these idioms is melodic rather than harmonic." Of the elision of implied resolutions he gives an example from Ravel's "Valses nobles et sentimentales," turning it into musical journalese by adding the resolutions, with an apology to the composer: " 'Your grasp of the obvious is painfully precise,' Ravel might say; and the remark would be just."

But would it? What the author does not seem quite to realise is the mechanical nature of all these harmonic complications, their routine use of mere rubber-stamp. It is at bottom Ravel, Debussy, and Scriabine who are painfully obvious, not Dr. Dyson's explanations of them. Formula is always obvious, once it is understood; and ultra-modern harmony is so largely the child of purely intellectualist formula that it is in reality infinitely more conventional than the classical harmony out of which it grew, in which emotion played a vital part. Dr. Dyson seems a bit timid, therefore, in carrying his own observations to their logical conclusions.

In contrast with his cautious qualifications Mr. Gray's headlong statements are sometimes refreshing, if not always strictly accurate. For instance, here is how he says virtually the same thing about Debussy. "His constant employment of common chords in parallelism [Dr. Dyson's "side-slip"] . . . is really not harmonic at all, but only a doubling of the melody in the third and fifth. . . . Few indeed among modern composers have actually progressed farther than the earliest tentative experiments of mediæval musicians; the principle on which their harmonic writing is based is, almost without exception, nothing but that of organum and its offspring *faux bourdon*—for it obviously makes little difference if seconds, sevenths, and ninths are thrown in with . . . mere thirds and sixths. . . . In his harmony Debussy is as curiously limited, monotonous, and restricted as in his melody."

He penetrates with equal ease the mask of harmonic complexity with which Ravel has sought to disguise the essential banality of his ideas, recognising that the "obviousness" is in the ideas themselves and that indeed Ravel's journalese is only made to look like literature by its highly polished surface. Commenting on the myth of Ravel's "absence of sensibility," he says: "He is actually an extremely sentimental little person who is only rather too ashamed to show it," and remarks: "Most professional cynics and ironists are like that, as a matter of fact." This is far nearer the mark than Dr. Dyson's deference, as is the later summing up: "Modern composers such as Debussy and Ravel have sought to attain to individuality through exclusion. . . . Mannerism and idiosyncrasy usurp the place of true individuality, which is not a surface quality, but an attribute of mind that can transform and impart significance to the most ordinary and even commonplace conceptions."

But to return to Dr. Dyson. Continuing his discussion of texture in a chapter on "Multiple Tonality" he makes some exceedingly acute generalizations. Of the immediate and remote influence of equal temperament he says: "When Beethoven modulated to a distant key he was compelled to leave part of his orchestra behind. When he returned, increased fulness of texture was unavoidably sudden. Effects of mass and of emphasis were thus fortified by classical practice. . . . Even now too many musicians appear to regard certain instruments as primarily the vehicles of a kind of super-splash in the harmonic fabric. . . . The vehemence to which such instruments can be excited . . . has been carried to a point with which only an African drummer can compete." Many curious results are deduced from three limitations of the piano:—that it has a percussive tone, that it is confined to a hand technique, and that it is intonation-proof. For instance: "Keyboard music, so far as it is unvocal, demands from the singer or orchestral player whose province it invades precisely that automatic and mechanical intonation which the keyboard provides. They have been educated to make their own notes. When they are asked to behave like automata, they are docile perhaps, but none the less bewildered. And this attitude goes deeper than the mere question of technique. Such music often finds capable performers. The pity is that it so rarely leaves them inspired." Here again Dr. Dyson seems to understate. It has been said that for the highly subdivided piecework of the modern factory, intelligence in a workman is almost a disqualification. It makes him restless; he would be happier and more efficient if he were a little sub-normal. In the same way it seems bad economy to set refined violinists or cellists sawing away on the music of Stravinsky. An orchestra of automata or robots would be cheaper, and less subject to human deviations from scientific accuracy.[1]

Far-reaching is Dr. Dyson's criticism of the theories of the most advanced chromaticists, particularly Busoni and Schönberg. He does well to make it clear at the outset that no amount of dissonance, in itself, will justify condemning such effects as theirs. "Let us admit at once," he says with admirable candor, "that

[1] Stravinsky is said to have praised Josef Hofmann in extravagant terms once for his performance of one of his pieces. The pianist's rising pleasure was somewhat damped when the composer continued: "Yes, you played it exactly as I wanted it—completely without expression."

the attempt to find a consistent physical basis for our impressions of consonance breaks down hopelessly. Ratios of vibration alone . . . will not account for the consonance to our ears of any of the harmonic systems actually in use. Equal temperament must have been excruciatingly painful to the hypersensitive, but the immediate wealth of melodic and harmonic expression that it offered overcame all opposition. Beauty in this matter is in the ear of the listener. It is an acquired taste, not an intuitive reaction."

The real dubiousness of the innovations proposed by Busoni in his "A Sketch of a New Æsthetic of Music," thinks Dyson, lies in their arbitrariness, in their intellectual rather than æsthetic origin. "To say that a new scale," he points out, "derived from an intellectual or arbitrary source, offers a field for musical expansion, is to state a hypothesis rather than a truth. Such a scale may indeed suggest to the sensitive imagination new relations, but it is only after the imagination has done its work, associating these new elements with the stored experiences of the mind and so fixing their relative significance, that they can become, even for the creator himself, vehicles of 'artistic' expression. And this is not enough. The hearer must have the same sense of values, or a capacity for experience that will enable him to evolve them, or the new dialect is meaningless."

If the relation of Busoni's fine-spun abstractions to the traditional values seem problematic to Dr. Dyson, he finds in Schönberg "a process of intellectualisation which has finally divorced expression from all traditional roots." Here is his summing up of certain quoted passages: "They have everything but meaning, as we have tried to define it. There is no interval or chord in them that cannot be found in works of classical derivation, but the definite orientation of an intelligible context which alone can give a system expressive values is to all appearances completely absent. There is no help for it. Significance is not absolute, but relative. 'When everybody's somebody, then no one's anybody.' If and when chromaticism has destroyed the conventional scales which gave it meaning, then it will either have to adopt new conventions or else die of aimlessness."

Mr. Gray, as has been suggested, is less thoughtful, methodical and analytic than Dr. Dyson, but he has moments of penetrating intuition, moments when he pierces the elaborate bluff of certain aspects of ultra-modernism as a child pierces the conventions of the adult dull. He is a sort of *enfant terrible* of musical criticism.

Here is his summing up of Scriabine:

"The main ingredients are clearly recognisable. First and foremost, one finds a kind of saccharine derived from the by-products of Chopin's consummate genius. Secondly, we get the element which operates the first fermentation in the music of Scriabine: an extract of diabolism carefully prepared from certain works of Liszt. Thirdly, appears a powerful aphrodisiac prepared from the monstrous flowers that grow in Klingsor's magic garden and in the scented caves of the Venusberg. These are the main ingredients, cemented together not by a strong, central nerve of personality, but by a kind of patent glucose or gelatine—a style with the flaccid, molluscular, invertebrate, viscid consistency of welsh rarebit."

And here is his summary of the most discussed musical personality of the hour:

"Stravinsky's only idea of form . . . is the old A-B-A formula, interspersed with occasional descriptive passages where the stage-action demands it; his only means of achieving continuity is by repeating whole bars and figures *ad nauseam et infinitum;* his only harmonic resource is to write simple sequences of thirds in different keys at the same time, or else to move about in blocks of notes according to the recipes of organum. His melodic invention is extraordinarily short and always monotonously pentatonic. In short, he has demonstrably none of the qualities of musicianship, except a remarkable orchestral virtuosity, and nothing grows stale so quickly. . . . No composer is less capable than he of writing music which can stand on its own legs, unsupported by the complicated paraphernalia of stage scenery, costumes, and dancing. That he of all people should claim to be regarded as a writer of pure music is one of the most remarkable examples of insolence and charlatanism in the history of art; that he should be accepted as one is only another instance of the melancholy stupidity and gullibility of the musical public."

How long-suffering this complaisance of the musical public may prove to be is an interesting question. Impatience with ultra-modernism has begun to make itself felt. There is widespread uneasiness, a revulsion, mostly inarticulate as

yet, but sullenly resolute, against the boredom
inflicted by its more relentlessly monotonous
features—against its primitive rhythms, its cluttered harmony, and its insignificant and banal
melody. Dr. Dyson's careful analysis and Mr.
Gray's spirited attacks do much to focus what
must on the whole be regarded as a wholesome
discontent.

VINCENT D'INDY IN AMERICA

THE visits to America, in one season,[1] of the foremost living composers of Germany and of France—Richard Strauss and Vincent d'Indy —irresistibly suggest certain comparisons between the musical arts of the two countries, as enlightening as they are paradoxical. A plausible case could be made for the theory that modern Germany and France, like two chemicals in a reaction, have exchanged elements, and reversed each other's character. Thus the realistic movement, or "program music" as it is more frequently called, beginning in France with Berlioz, passed through Liszt into Germany, where it finds its greatest contemporary representative in Strauss. During this same period, moreover, while "tone painting" was thus being transmitted from the naturally literary and dramatic French to the more subjective and emotional Germans, the other type of music, which, to distinguish it from the outward-looking art of the scene-painter, we may call "inward-looking" or "pure" music—this older

[1] 1921-1922.

type, born in the land of *innigkeit* and so gloriously nurtured by Beethoven, Schubert, Schumann and Brahms, crossed the Rhine in the
other direction, established itself in Paris
through the labors of the half-Teutonic Bel-
gian, César Franck, and finds possibly its most
eloquent living representative in the highly Gallic Vincent d'Indy. Thus, while the symphonic
poem, born in France, was reaching a resplen-
dent maturity in Germany, its older brother, the
symphony, had quietly emigrated from its native land and was enjoying in France a new
lease of unexpected life.

As long ago as 1905, M. Romain Rolland
clearly described these tendencies.

> German music [he wrote], is daily losing its in-
> timate spirit; there are still traces of this spirit in Wolf,
> thanks to his exceptionally unhappy life; but there is
> very little of it in Mahler, in spite of all his efforts
> to concentrate his mind on himself; and there is hardly
> any at all in Strauss, although he is the most interesting
> of the three composers. German composers have no
> longer any depth.

In the score of years since these words were
written their truth has been strikingly corroborated by the career of Strauss. He has become

constantly more brilliantly external. In his early works, brilliant externality gave place to moments at least of introspection and pure beauty. In "Death and Transfiguration," despite its cruel realism in the depiction of the death-struggle, the panting for breath, the intolerable tension of pain, there is the sweet innocence of the childhood music, there is the grandeur of the theme of transfiguration. In "Till Eulenspiegel" the literal episodes in the life of the ingratiating rogue which make the body of the work are idealised and grasped in their essential human spirit in the prologue and epilogue, in which, as in the last of Schumann's "Childhood Scenes," "the poet speaks." Even in the "Sinfonia Domestica" there is the magnificently imaginative treatment of the Husband-theme to offset the puerile futilities of the squalling baby, as in the "Hero's Life" there is the love music to make up for those silly "Adversaries." But from about the time of the "Hero's Life" the tendency towards literal scene-painting, towards a crass and vulgar materialism, which Mr. Ernest Newman has so skilfully analysed, gained steadily on the better elements in Strauss, until we have the *reductio ad absurdum* of his method in the "Alpine Sym-

phony," with its sorry inanities of stage-car-
pentered sunrises, "real" cowbells and imitation
thunder, unredeemed by any true emotional
penetration of the sentiment of mountains. In
this work, with its extravagant luxury of
means, its pathetic spiritual poverty, Strauss
is at last pitilessly revealed as, in Mr. Paul
Rosenfeld's phrase, "the false dawn of modern
music."

But is the true dawn to be found any more in
France than in Germany? M. Rolland thought
in 1905 that it was.

At this German music festival [he said], it was a
Frenchman [César Franck] who represented not only
serious music moulded in a classical form, but a religious spirit. The characters of two nations have been
reversed. The Germans have so changed that they
are only able to appreciate this seriousness and religious faith with difficulty. I watched the audience
on this occasion; they listened politely, a little aston-
ished and bored, as if to say, 'What business has this
Frenchman with depth and piety of soul?' . . . It was
only the other day that German music enjoyed the
privilege of boring us in France.

If M. Rolland were writing today he would
probably be obliged to admit that the Franck-

ists now "enjoy the privilege of boring" not only the Germans, but many of their compatriots; and this would be an admission damaging not to the Franckists but to modern French taste.

Have not France and the rest of Europe, in fact, the false emphasis of war-propaganda to the contrary notwithstanding, been about as much debased as Germany itself by the materialism, growing ever more mad for thirty years before 1914, that was the true cause of the war? Modern France would seem, to an unprejudiced observer, as would modern America for that matter, about as materialistic as modern Germany. To such an observer, Franckism appears, unfortunately, as only an oasis of vitalism in a desert of materialism and its by-products, a small group inspired by faith outclamored by a disillusioned herd. Of the three other groups in clique-ridden France which struggle with this forlorn hope for supremacy, each bears the mark clearly enough of our world-wide modern materialism, either in fulfilment of it or in reaction against it. The impressionism of which Debussy was the leader was in part a wholesome revolt against the megalomania of Strauss, Mahler and

Reger, an assertion eminently Gallic of the superiority of quality to quantity, of distinction to size, of refinement to brute force. But it was also, less happily, with its emphasis on sensuous charm, its retirement to the ivory tower, a confession of the spiritual exhaustion which materialism brings in its train. Debussy has been especially successful, as has been pointed out elsewhere, "in his appeal to the modern preference of sensation to thought and emotion, of subjective day-dreaming to the impersonal perception of beauty." [2] In these preferences he has, of course, many more sympathisers in contemporary France than has d'Indy in his austerer ideal of thought and emotion embodied in objective beauty.

The fatigue of modern life has led to another kind of reaction in the reversion to barbaric stimuli of modern primitives like Stravinsky, Schmitt and the other devotees of dance-rhythms and the pantomime. Exhausted nerves, minds rendered incapable, by the distractions and useless complications of our machinery, of concentrating themselves upon the syntheses of sensation that are required by gen-

[2] "Contemporary Composers," by Daniel Gregory Mason; page 139.

uine art, fall back on the crude sensations themselves. It is strange and somewhat repulsive to see European musicians, with long and intensive culture behind them, at the behest of tired nerves throwing it all away and acclaiming American ragtime, the sweepings of our streets, as the rejuvenator of their senile art. Even stranger is the arid intellectualism that in those whose emotions are dead, or never lived, gives birth to all manner of fads and fashions based upon formulæ. Those who, like Erik Satie and the "Six," try to substitute process and idiom for the living instincts out of which alone real art is made, are another kind of victims of materialism, victims of its languor, its ennui and disillusion, breeding irony, self-consciousness and unwillingness to risk a loyalty. . . . No, modern France is not a good place for a vitalist. It is a wilderness of impressionism, barbarism, and intellectualism. Vincent d'Indy is a voice crying in that wilderness, and his cry is: *"Il n'est vraiment, en art, que le cœur pour engendrer de la beauté."* At over seventy, despite his imposing reputation, which few trouble to understand, and surrounded by a small group of friends more of whom are sentimental idolators than intelligent supporters, and by many enemies (for he is a well-hated man), Vincent d'Indy is perhaps more alone than ever. Yet there is power in that solitude, for he has with him the truth. *"Il n'est que le cœur pour engendrer de la beauté."*

Born in Paris in 1851 of an aristocratic and strongly Roman Catholic family, Vincent d'Indy became a pupil of César Franck in 1873, and through the Société Nationale of which he became president after Franck's death in 1890, and the Schola Cantorum, a music school strongly impregnated with the principles of plain chant, which he founded with Alexander Guilmant and Charles Bordes in 1896, has done more than any other one man to disseminate the Franck spirit, both in creation and in education. Among his works are three symphonies and the beautiful program symphony "A Summer Day on the Mountain," "Istar: Symphonic Variations," and several smaller orchestral works; for chamber music, a violin sonata, and two string quartets; the cantata "Chant de la Cloche"; and three works for the stage, "Fervaal," "L'Etranger," and "La Legende de St. Christophe," the latter a *"drame sacré"* occupying in his work somewhat the position that "Parsifal" does in Wagner's. D'Indy has been indefatigable also as a teacher, conductor, editor, and writer. His best-known books are his life of César Franck and his monumental treatise, "Cours de Composition Musicale," not yet completed.

It is interesting to compare his program symphony, "A Summer Day on the Mountain," with Strauss's "Alpine Symphony." The French master, who is a devout lover of mountains, contents himself with comparatively few suggestions of external nature. In the first movement, "Dawn," there is the empty blankness of the mist before sunrise, the twittering of birds, the gradually increasing light and animation suggested by changes of key and rhythm, the final gorgeous appearance of the sun in a blaze of B major. In the second movement, "Day—Afternoon Under the Pines," we have almost no tone-painting, but rather an unforgettable evocation of the mood of the scene and place. Then come realistic suggestions of a peasant's song in the valley, and later a sort of marching theme—perhaps a regiment going by. In the last movement, "Evening," there is first the animation of full day; then gradually an abatement, an almost imperceptible darkening and saddening, and a lovely melody that is like a song as one goes home at evening, a song profoundly characteristic of d'Indy, full of happy serenity and devout thankfulness. Then gradually the shades descend, the passages early in the symphony suggestive of mist and half-light recur, there is faint clashing of chimes in the distance, and after the song of thankfulness has been sung once more a heavenly passage made from a variant of the theme of full day, in which all is calmed and quieted to the mood of dusk. It is hard to listen to such a passage without tears; for it is not sticks and stones that it gives us, but the very accent of what this beauty of the darkening day means to a responsive spirit.

For all his solitude in a Paris largely given to fads and fashions, and to the pursuit of what is called "originality," Vincent d'Indy impresses one as tranquil and content. He has the French knack of discounting enmity by understanding it, and even by ironically rallying it. In his "Legende de St. Christophe," there is an amusing scene wherein are introduced in succession "Les Faux Penseurs," "Les Faux Savants," "Une Foule Nombreuse et Burlante," "Les Arrivistes Orgueilleux," and "Les Faux Artistes."

The false artists proclaim and condemn themselves as follows:

"Falsifiers of an art fine and rare,
We make the fashion, and we follow it.
Let everything be pulled down to our stature.
Hatred to enthusiasm!
Hatred to ideal art!
No more rules! No more study!
Let us be little, let us be original."

Better still than irony, however, is the calm religious faith, the Christian confidence in all that is permanent and good in life, that sustains this priest of beauty and love in a world so largely given over to ugliness and hatred. As one talks with d'Indy about the eccentricities and perversities that make up so much of our modern artistic activity, one gradually loses the hatred of them that comes from fear, one catches a little of his tolerance and quizzical amusement, one goes back as he has gone to Bach, Beethoven, Franck—that august stream of beauty which comes down through ages, washing away with it so much temporary jetsam too flimsily made, and one finally remembers only a sentence that one heard from him many years ago, and that obviously sustains him now in his old age as it armed him then in the struggles of his prime: *"Les principes d'art sont éternelles; ils restent."*

REFLECTIONS ON RHYTHM

I

OWING to fundamental differences in the media of the three arts, the rhythmic subtleties possible to music are probably not appreciated by most poets and painters. Poetry and music, indeed, alike differing from painting in the use of audible rather than visual rhythms, with all the psychological peculiarities thus implied, differ again between themselves in the degree to which their auditory space may be subdivided, music being able because of its accurate system of meter to divide it much more minutely and variously than poetry, which must rest content with more massive effects. But both are more dependent on that accurate division into equal units, as a groundwork for later elaboration, which we call meter, than is painting. This is probably due to the basic difference between perception by the ear and perception by the eye. While the eye can run back and forth freely over the field of its visual space, correcting and verifying its impressions at need, the ear can proceed easily in only one direction, from past to future, and if comparison or verification is needed can go the other way, from future to past, only by the aid of memory, necessarily far fainter and less reliable than perception. Hence it is perhaps that the ear has to go more heedfully than the eye, and finds almost indispensable a meter of equal units to help it apprehend clearly, and before they pass by, its unequal objects. If the eye could proceed only from left to right over the surface of a picture, such a regular meter of visual space might also be found helpful in perceiving and fixating significant irregularities of shape. Indeed it may be questioned whether we do not, even as it is, subconsciously divide visual space to some extent into equal units in the process of apprehending unequal shapes, as where, for instance, the horizon in a landscape is almost exactly at two-thirds or at three-fourths of the height of the picture.

Whatever our procedure with visual space, there can be no doubt that the disadvantage the ear suffers under in being able to move in only one direction practically compels us to guide it across its auditory space by laying down thereon equal units—groups of syllables of unequal stress for poetry, of beats of unequal stress for music, making up in their regular serial succession what we call meter. The unchanging regularity of these metric schemes is not a limitation, as careless theorists and iconoclasts have sometimes hastily assumed, but a supreme merit, because a *sine qua non* of their performing their function. Unless meter is systematic, rhythm cannot be significant; irregularity, as the very etymology of the word shows, is inconceivable save as a negation of regularity, just as error is conceivable only if there is a truth from which it errs; and it would seem that in the freest of free verse there must be suggested a metrical pulse, just as in the most syncopated music there must be occasionally a regular accent, or the mind will lose its bearings. While the *vers-librists* are entirely right in condemning sing-song (with its musical analogues of trivial short rhythms and the *phrase carrée*) and in demanding a vital flexibility in the ultimate rhythms, they confuse rather than emancipate us in so far as they ignore the function of meter as a necessarily regular basis for the interesting rhythmic irregularities. The same is true of those composers, like Mr. Cyril Scott for instance, who vary their time-signatures whimsically and per-

148

versely with every measure, so that the mind of the listener is baffled in its search for reference-points. The effect of such a jumble is not in reality various at all, but highly monotonous because unintelligible. Real variety is always a gradation from subordination to salience in the parts of the objects, shapes, or, as we call them in music, the "motives," superimposed on uniform units of measurement (beats or measures).

When Pope noted of the poetry of some of his uninspired contemporaries

"And ten low words oft creep in one dull line"

his satire was not in the least aimed at the iambic pentameter, which he used throughout his life, but at the lack of musical sense which could so abuse it. When he wrote his own line

"Drink deep, or taste not the Pierian spring"

he gave an excellent example in that "Pierian" of how significant word-patterns give vitality to rhythm, pulling away accents from where the meter alone would lead us to expect them, and thus setting up an opposition between dead meter and living rhythm which it is perhaps not too fanciful to compare with the opposition between dead chemical elements and their living compounds in our organisms, by which life is precariously sustained. We see the same thing in music when we compare a "one dull line" like the tune of "Yankee Doodle" with the festoon of vital rhythm, flinging itself freely over the measure without ever violating it, and yet without ever becoming servile to it, of a really fine tune like "Dixie." Always the rhythm builds freely, irregularly, on the meter, but always the regular, systematic meter must be there to build upon.

May it not be that the superior subtlety of musical over poetic rhythms may thus be due to the more rigorous systematisation and more minute subdivision of meter possible in music? Is not poetry always a little more in danger of obliterating a meter by a rhythm and so spoiling the rhythm itself? Is not the essential distinction between accent (dynamic stress) and value (time stress) harder to preserve? It is true that modern poetry can sublimate even the iambic pentameter to far more subtle beauties than that of Pope's line, as E. A. Robinson, for instance, does here:

"For I would have you glad that I still keep
Your memory, and even at the end—
Impenitent, sick, shattered—cannot curse
The love that flings, for better or for worse,
This worn-out, cast-out flesh of mine to sleep."

—It is true that it can even mix different types
of meter, for example the dactyls of

"Come to me, dearest, I'm lonely without thee"

with the anapests of

"The Assyrian came down like a wolf on the fold."

so that it would no doubt be possible to put
"crocodile" and "cigarette" in the same line
and preserve their metric values. But music
can do more. It can maintain anapests and
dactyls *simultaneously* in two voices, thus rendering contrapuntally a contrast that poetry can
only work out melodically; and it can also, even
in simple alternations, preserve the individual
flavor of the different metric groups better
through its more accurate time-measurement
and stress.

While its regularly recurring accents on the
first beats of measures—on the "Ones"—is
thus an indispensable means to its subtlest

151

rhythmic effects, however, it carries with it the peculiar danger of an over-obviousness when these "Ones" became too insistent or too unrelieved. Hence the instinctive interest of all sensitive composers in all means for disguising, so long as disguise does not obliterate, this relentless and necessary pulse. One means is the suppression of actual notes on such accents, suggesting rather than expressing them. "Empty first beats" are immensely effective in piano and in chamber music, less so in orchestral music, where the players, less independent and hence less responsible, are less likely to play with conviction unless they "hear a One." Ingenious composers resort to many devices to give them this necessary *"point d'appui"* outside of the essential melodic and harmonic texture, as by kettle-drum or cymbal strokes, plucked notes for strings, harp notes, or *sforzandos* for the horns.

Another means of keeping meter definite without letting it become monotonous is the systematic alternation of varying measures, a familiar instance of which is Tschaikowsky's famous five-beat time in his Pathetic Symphony, in reality a fixed alternation of twos and threes. Rachmaninoff, in his "Island of the Dead," refines on this by using a five which is sometimes two plus three and at other times three plus two, always carefully indicating which in the score. Arensky, in his delightful "Studies in Forgotten Rhythms," has used even more complex compounds, and there is no limit to what may be done with such measures as three-plus-two-plus-three (a radically different thing from eight) and two-plus-three-plus-two, a fascinating form of seven.[1] The future will doubtless see such meters much developed, more than they have been in a period too much obsessed with the search for mere harmonic singularity, a lower kind of interest. In all these experiments, however, it will have to be remembered that some kind of metric regularity is essential, as the unchanging groundwork on which the composer's imagination drapes or flings those festoons of vital, and therefore irregular, rhythmic melody which are the ultimate reality of music.

II

To what degree is good taste in the listener dependent on the sense of rhythm? Is it pos-

[1] See the trio of the Scherzo in the present writer's Quartet for Piano and Strings, opus 7, and the Caprice in his Three Pieces for Flute, Harp, and String Quartet, opus 13.

sible for those in whom this sense is deficient, either by nature or from lack of training, to cultivate it? How would such cultivation, if under the spur of enthusiasm for beauty it were widely undertaken, affect the attitude of audiences toward various types of music, such, for example, as the music of Bach, Wagner, or Brahms, or toward fads like ultra-modernism and jazz? On such interesting and important questions a good deal of light may be thrown by certain psychological considerations concerning rhythm.

First of all it is well to remember how fundamental and pervasive an element is rhythm, not only of music but of all art, how protean and many-sided are its aspects, and consequently how misleading are those fussily technical definitions of it that really obscure rather than clarify it, because they emphasise its letter at the expense of its spirit. Vincent d'Indy's definition is serviceable in the degree of its generality: "Rhythm is order and proportion in space and in time." Rhythm is indeed the basis of all types of art: well said von Bülow: "In the beginning was rhythm." Spatial order and proportion are nobly exemplified in the arrangement of columns, windows, friezes and other

154

architectural elements in some perfect building like the Parthenon, or in a beautiful pictorial composition like Titian's "Young Man with the Glove." In music and poetry, the time arts, we find the same order and proportion in the grouping, in ever higher hierarchies, of words and tones, of feet and measures, of lines and phrases, of stanzas and tunes, of cantos and movements, all going to make up the complete poem or symphony. Wherever, in short, a number of similar elements, such as windows in architecture, syllables, words, or phrases in poetry, notes, motives or melodies in music, are so ordered and proportioned that they become a unity, there is rhythm.

Moreover it is evident not only that rhythm is active on a great many different levels, so to speak, in any single art such as music, but that its effectuation requires the active participation of the listener, and that different listeners differ strikingly in the amount of participation they are capable of giving.[2] Tom may be able to group notes into phrases, but not phrases into complete tunes; Dick may perceive the tunes, but not their coördination within the whole

[2] See "Ears to Hear," by the present writer, a pamphlet issued by the American Library Association.

movement; Harry may miss the still wider synthesis of the movements in the whole symphony. Hence music is in a very real sense at the mercy of audiences. If audiences had always been made up of South Sea Islanders, Beethoven could never have existed; if the craze for jazz and similar crudities should become universal, truly beautiful music would become extinct. Fortunately such crazes are always highly ephemeral.

Now a peculiarity of music and poetry, as time arts, is that this active process of perception (or, to use the exact psychological term, "apperception") by which we take them into our minds, takes place, as d'Indy also points out, from the particular to the general, while in the space arts it moves the other way, from the general to the particular. If we examine, he says, a cathedral, such as Notre Dame de Paris, it is "a magnificent ensemble, a general line harmonised in beauty, an aspect of majesty in proportion, that strike us first. Then analysing it, we discover little by little all the details: columns, pillars, doors, windows and those admirable statues of the outer galleries, hardly visible from the pavement, but all contributing to the primary impression of the ensemble. . . .

Let us listen now," proceeds d'Indy, "to a symphony, say Beethoven's Fifth, and what is it that we hear in the first place? A detail"—he quotes the four notes of the "Fate knocking at the door" motive—"a particular and precise design to which our mind attaches itself, an idea that we follow with interest through all its development up to its final flowering. Memory, constantly busy during this work of assimilation, recalls to us the principal idea each time it recurs under a new aspect, and we thus raise ourselves progressively to the synthetic impression of the ensemble, by the successive perception of details." [3]

In poetry and music, in other words, our sense of rhythm works from moment to moment, from detail to detail, and builds up wholes from these details only gradually. Furthermore, it is evident that individuals differ enormously in the power of building up rhythms synthetically—differ in native aptitude, in the development of it through persistent experience, and even in momentary nervous condition —and that these differences are crucial to taste. In a general way, high synthetic power seems

[3] Vincent d'Indy, "Cours de composition musicale," Volume I, page 17.

to be a chief element in the formation of "good" or distinguished taste, while low synthetic power (or of course inattentiveness, which comes to the same thing) reveals itself in "bad" or vulgar taste. If we adopt the psychologists' term "span of apperception" for measuring the synthetic power, we may safely say that good taste is that of the people of wide apperceptive span, vulgar taste that of people of narrow span. In poetry, for instance, narrow span shows itself in inability to pass easily from the unit of the foot to the larger units of lines or groups of lines, and in the consequent preference for obvious sing-song rhythms where all the feet are alike to more subtle and irregular groupings, so much more beautiful to a mind of wider span.

In music we find the same reflection of rudimentary powers in the wide popularity of jazz. Jazz is a sort of musical doggerel, devoid of broad or truly beautiful rhythm, all cut up into snippets of a few notes each, which the narrowest span can catch. Therefore it appeals to two types of listeners: first, those whose mentality is innately low, or undeveloped by an intelligent effort to understand real music; second, those who, though capable of better things,

158

are momentarily tired or bored, as so many of us are in modern cities. Attempts have been made to find in jazz the "artistic expression" of our industrial age. This is sadly to misread the connection which undoubtedly exists between jazz and industrialism. Industrialism has produced widespread fatigue: fatigue craves exaggerated physical stimuli combined with a minimum appeal to the mind. Jazz provides both of these, and is accordingly the music of the jaded. . . . In that horribly impressive play, "R. U. R.," in which the mechanised automatons ("robots") men had invented to carry on their industries, were shown revolting against their masters, and finally massacring them, a woman was heard, during a pause in the preparations for resisting their attack, playing in an adjoining room a Chopin nocturne. Strangely poignant was its suggestion of human aspiration, imperfection, and irregularity against this inhuman background of relentless mechanical "efficiency." Surely, if robots could make a music of their own, it would be jazz.

A really beautiful melody, such as it takes a Chopin, a Schumann, or a Brahms to create, exacts (and rewards), in the listener, a wide apperceptive span. You cannot "get" a melody of Brahms by half a dozen jerks of attention, any more than you can see the Parthenon through a small auger-hole. Brahms is an especially good case in point, because we have many of us had the experience of actively disliking, at first, themes of his we later came to love. We had in fact just the sort of difficulty that psychological experiment has shown school children to have with poets of fine rhythmic feeling such as Masefield or Shelley.[4] It is the same difficulty that a reader accustomed to very even iambic pentameters such as Pope's might have with freer rhythms, such as those already cited from E. A. Robinson.

He who would appreciate the highest beauties must learn to apperceive by large groups, by lines rather than feet, by long sweeping phrases rather than by jazz-like rattles of a few notes. The inevitable effect of such wider grasp is to subordinate details more and more in a larger hierarchy, and hence to make ever fewer accents. Needless accent is as vulgar in music as superlatives are in speech, and for the same reason—that they betray a lack of intelligent sense of proportion. In interpreters (notably in pianists, in whom, alas, it is seldom

[4] See "Stravinsky as a Symptom."

found) a crucial test of distinction is broad and quiet phrasing, freedom from distracting choppy accentuation, just as a crucial test of good manners is quietness. And so it is with music itself. What music is it that requires as little accent as possible, and is so ruined by unnecessary accent that playing it, to those trained in our feverish post-Wagnerian modern music, is almost a lost art?—Mozart. . . . And what music is it that not only tolerates quite superfluous accents, but positively makes a fetish of them, putting in two or three where one grew before?—Jazz. . . . Further comment is unnecessary.

THE TYRANNY OF THE BAR-LINE

I

A WELL-KNOWN piano teacher tells a
story of a prospective pupil who played
him, after apologies for incomplete preparation, a horrible hodge-podge, and explained that
she always learned her pieces first "without the
sharps and flats" and "put them in afterwards."
Few people are as naïve as that; but we have
all met (and unfortunately heard) performers
who regard what they call "interpretation" or
"expression" as something extraneous to the
music, a movable commodity, to be put in afterwards, like the young lady's sharps and flats.
First, they think, you play the notes—they are
primary; then, as an afterthought, you "put in"
the expression as the cook adds the seasoning
to the dish, or you apply it to the surface as the
cabinet-maker applies the varnish. Seldom, on
the other hand, do they thus subordinate bril-
liancy of execution; probably far more performers are drawn to their work by physical
skill than by any great sense of beauty or

162

meaning in music; hence, to the misfortune of the art, the virtuosos greatly outnumber the artists.

The opposition between virtuosity and art is usually moral as well as æsthetic, so that the choice every performer has to make between them is affected by the maturity of his mind. Virtuosity, pursued for itself, is essentially show and its motive not only an innocent pleasure in skill but a less desirable personal vanity. Art is communication, an activity essentially social and impersonal. And as everyone naturally evolves from the personal to the impersonal view only slowly and painfully if at all, it is inevitable that the young student should try at first merely to "show off," and should need the sympathy, intelligence, and contagious idealism of the teacher to help him to a better point of view. Teachers should therefore never cease to insist on this fundamental opposition of virtuosity and art, should mercilessly bring it home to pupils that their own vanity is the chief obstacle to their becoming true, however humble, artists, and should urge them to apply constantly for themselves this discrimination to all who are before the public, and to learn the chastening lesson of why there are so few artists among the hordes of showmen, mercenaries, and self-exploiters.

Closely akin to the absurd idea that expression is superficial, to be put on and off like a glove, is the equally widespread one that it is peculiar to the individual artist, and more or less waywardly adopted by him. We often hear conductors' "interpretations" of well-known works spoken of as if they were necessarily unique, as if it would be as monstrous for two conductors to find the same interpretation as to marry the same woman. In one sense, of course, this is true, since no one can prevent his peculiarities from more or less coloring all that he does. But speaking broadly, this notion of "interpretation" as a sort of personal kink or twist is altogether mischievous, and comparable to that fetish of "originality" which is one of the banes of art. It is only the little minds that strain always to be "original"; the great ones are too interested observing and expressing and making to bother about it. So-called "originality" is far less vital to artists of all kinds, reproductive as well as productive, than wide human contacts, broad sanity, representative power. In the same way, it is only the charlatans or the mountebanks that distort

164

a work of art in order to set their personal stamp upon it; the real interpreters are aiming not at distortion but at just proportion; at centrality, not eccentricity.

"Interpretation," in short, comes on analysis to mean something far deeper than the self-exhibition of the virtuoso, something far more organic than the expression added "like sharps and flats," something more fundamental and far-reaching than the whims of the devotee of originality. It comes to mean nothing less than the art of making music intelligible to the universal mind. This art is a perfectly definite and to some extent communicable one, involving certain principles capable of formulation—though of course it cannot be reduced entirely to rules any more than any other living art.

II

Every musical phrase may be conceived as a shape or design, a tonal profile, so to speak, which has to be projected to the mind of the hearer through his ear alone, without any help from his eyes, touch, or other senses. While the performer can see the printed music, and is guided by its visual divisions (measures, phrases, sections, and the like) the hearer cannot, but must depend on his unaided ear. The performer has therefore to project to him these profiles, and has no means at command save gradations of sound. He can graduate the sounds both as regards stress or accent and as regards duration (with its psychological effect of stress), but that is all he can do. Upon his success in outlining his rhythms clearly by means of such gradations of stress and duration will depend the eloquence of his interpretation. These considerations help us to understand the force of von Bülow's saying: "In the beginning was rhythm"; for rhythmic relations are literally basic in determining the intelligibility and emotional appeal of all performance. It will always be found on analysis that great performance owes its ability to carry us along with it, to set us tingling and thrilling with excitement, primarily to its solid, well-articulated, flexible and various rhythmic scheme, and that *per contra* vapid, dull performance, such as we hear not only from amateurs but from many professionals, including even orchestral conductors of national fame, is always unvitalised rhythmically—either flabby and inert, or, what comes to the same thing, exaggerated and over-emphasised.

The weakness of overemphasis may remind us that the keynote of the whole situation is proper subordination. Stevenson said that if he only knew what to omit he could make a classic out of a daily paper; and in the same way we could give musical eloquence to the strumming of the veriest tyro if we could induce him to subordinate. It is a great error to suppose that emphasis is positive, a matter of harder hitting. The more you pound, the less you express. The technique of emphasis is negative; you have to know what to omit, what to hold back, what to slur over. The pianist's monotonous *forte* is no more convincing than the schoolgirl's superlatives, and her "wonderful" and "marvellous"; it can no more give us audible shapes than a picture all lights and no shades can give us visual ones. In short, tonal dynamics are not absolute but relative; and as human capacity is limited we must take a hint from Chopin, who, physically unable to play *fortissimo*, yet made the effect by contrasting his *forte* with an exquisite *pianissimo* and with many shades between, and get our emphasis not by loudening the loud but by softening the soft, or as a painter would say, get our values not by brightening the high lights but by darkening

167

the shades. In working out the actual details of such subordination we shall find, first, that at every level of musical organisation from that of beats into measures up to that of themes into complete pieces the principle of subordinating the unimportant to the important holds good; and second, that the values of each level must in turn be subordinated as a whole to those of higher levels. These two principles seem to be the most important that we can discover as to interpretation.

The principle of the subordination of the unimportant to the important on any given level—for instance, of light beats to heavy in meter, or of short or passing notes to long or pivotal notes in rhythm—is so completely familiar in theory, even to the point of boresome truism, that we are often tempted to take it for granted in performance. But if we do we make a serious error. For it is surprising how many fairly good, or at least fairly experienced, professional musicians subordinate unintelligently or hardly at all, never outgrowing the relentless insistence on the indifferent which they probably fell into as children. The cellist of a well-known New York string quartet plays

the bass of the Trio in the Polka of Smetana's
Quartet "Aus Meinem Leben" like this:

Figure VII

That is hardly an exaggeration. By this ele-
phantine treading on secondary beats and frac-
tions of beats the player manages completely
to vulgarise Smetana's charming rhythm:

Figure VIII

A professional pianist once seriously argued that as the "rain-drops" in Chopin's Prelude are all eighth notes they should be precisely equal in accent, like this:

Figure IX

Rain-drops! They sounded more like hail-stones, or hand-grenades. It is like the school-boy's conscientious emphasis on all the "ofs," "ons" and "thes" in "The boy stood on the burning deck." If you listen to an artist, such as Gabrilowitsch for instance, play the prelude, you will be struck by the way he brings most of those A-flats near to the vanishing point. Here as elsewhere, any stress that is not neces-sary is worse than useless, is positively injurious to clearness of outline.

The national anthem, "My Country, 'tis of Thee" (or "God Save the King"), is usually written in quarter notes, and in 3-4 measure, as at A in Figure X. It has immeasurably

Figure X

My coun - try 'tis of thee Sweet land of

lib - er - ty, Of thee I sing

more dignity and repose if written in 3-2 measure as at B. What are the reasons for this striking change of effect?—all the more striking in that the notes remain identically the same in time-value, all that is changed being the metrical grouping and rhythmic outline. The declamation has something to do with it, no doubt. Neither version, unfortunately, avoids the superfluous strong accent on "'tis"; but while the 3-4 makes us say *"My* country, *'tis* of thee, *Sweet* land of *lib*erty, *Of* thee I *sing*"—which is about as wrong as it could be—the 3-2, emphasising the key words *country, thee, land, liberty, thee,* and *sing,* gives us the obviously far more just: "My *country 'tis* of *thee,* Sweet *land* of *lib*erty, Of *thee* I *sing.*"

But there is something even deeper than declamation at stake (capital as that is) and that something seems to be the too great proportion of accented to non-accented notes in the first version. The "sing-songiness" of it is due to regular almost dance-like recurrence of accent, while the greater dignity of the second version seems to be partly due to its freer, more leisurely flow. Mere pace is not so determining as one might think. No matter how pompously you pound out A it remains essentially trivial, and B can be taken fairly fast without becoming wholly ignoble.

In whichever way the tune is written, however, performance can do much to make it more or less impressive. Doubtless the way to make it completely unendurable is to write it in 3-4 and then accent every first beat—in other words, to adopt an obvious meter and then sacrifice the rhythm to the meter: and this brings us to our second principle, the subordination of

lower to higher levels of organisation, and the
common violation of it due to what we may call
the tyranny of the bar-line.

III

Every musician of experience, every teacher,
every performer, above all every orchestral
conductor, is familiar with what might be
termed the paradox of meter—namely, that
without meter (that is to say, the definite grouping of beats in measures, regulated by accents)
there can be no rhythm, and yet that, on the
other hand, meter is a dangerous enemy of
rhythm. The smaller grouping we call meter
must precede and support the larger grouping
we call rhythm; at the same time the least over-
insistence on the measure-group, the least rigid-
ity in its interpretation, destroys rhythm. Furthermore, the metrical grouping is constantly
and unmistakably suggested to the eye by the
bar-lines, while there is no such tangible re-
minder of the larger and far more important
punctuation of the musical sentence into
phrases. The result is that soloists and conductors frequently fall victims to this tyranny
of the bar-line, and give us tonal pictures in
which the essential contours are sacrificed to

the separate spots of paint, so to speak—pictures hopelessly "out of drawing."

Psychologically considered, meter and rhythm are both groupings of impressions instinctively made in the interest of ease and clearness of perception. Instead of perceiving each beat by a separate mental act we group either two or three beats together, accenting one in order to give the group a nucleus. Thus arises the simple measure, duple or triple. If a beat is, in turn, divided into several tones we group these again by giving a slighter accent to the first. Compound measures we perceive as groups of two or more simple measures bound together by an additional accent at the beginning. There is thus a hierarchy of accents from slight to heavy, corresponding with the increasing span of the units to be grouped, the heaviest accents coming at the beginnings of the measures, and therefore immediately after the bar-lines. Heavy accentuation thus comes by inveterate habit to be associated in our minds with the bar-line—with results disastrous to our interpretations unless modified by more important perceptions.

The process of grouping does not stop with the measure. As Riemann, Prout and others

174

have shown theoretically, and as every good ear
feels instinctively, measures in turn are apt to
feel "heavy" or "light" according to their place
in the organism of the phrase.   And even the
organisation of phrases into larger groups may
depend to some extent, especially if the tempo
is at all fast, on accent.   All this may be made
clear by an example.   The opening phrases of

Figure XI

Beethoven's Fifth Symphony will depend for
their clearness, to a hearer who sees neither the
music nor the beat of the conductor, on a whole

series of accent-systems, which may be set down
theoretically (though in performance, as we
shall see, they are modified by other considerations) as follows:

Beginning just above the printed notes (see
Figure XI), and rising as we proceed, let us
set down a separate line of accents for each
grade of organisation, metrical and rhythmical.

The first series shows the grouping of two
eighth notes in the quarter-note beat; the second, directly above it, the grouping of beats
in measures; the third, the alternation of heavy
and light measures; the fourth, the moulding
of all four measures into the single phrase; the
fifth, the opposition of principal and subordinate phrase, or, in the more usual terminology,
antecedent and consequent. Of course, not all
these accents would actually be made in performance; the object of the figure is rather to
arrive at a mathematically exact notion of the
relative force of the various accents, provided
they were all to be observed literally.

The result of the calculation is to show that
the important points in this passage are those
where we find, respectively, five, four and three
of the superposed accents. Play it with carefully graduated stresses at these points, and

you secure the greatest possible clearness and
force. But these accents, it will be observed,
are one and all rhythmical, not metrical. What
is the effect here of observing jealously the metrical accents (the two lowermost series)?
What is the effect, in other words, of submitting to the tyranny of the bar-line? Is it not
precisely to ruin the elasticity of the music, to
paralyse its movement and to distort its outline? To accent the beginning of each measure
is to make the passage stiff, mechanical, essentially unrhythmical. In short, there are accents
and accents; the metrical are of a lower order
than the rhythmical, and must give way before
them; to insist meticulously on the measure may
be to spoil the phrase.

This over-insistence on the metrical accent to
the injury of phrase outline is not a bugaboo
created by the critical imagination; it is an
actual and common fault in singing, piano-
playing, conducting. How often do we hear
the fluid ebb and flow of the rhythms of great
masters frozen by too rigid a conception of
meter! The effect is like that of the recitation
of children, who read word by word instead of
in phrases. It is like the speaking of a foreign
language of which we understand the separate

words but not their modes of crystallising. Or again, it is like looking at a picture too near; we get merely the detail, we miss those large contours, those intelligible shapes, which may be seen only at a distance. The small group must in every case be absorbed in the larger, not because it is unimportant on its own level, but because to a wider view it becomes subordinate, and must fall proportionately into the background.

What makes the matter still more vital is that while the meter often remains the same through long sections, if not the whole, of a piece, the rhythms are constantly changing; meter supplies uniformity of time division, rhythm supplies variety. Hence over-insistence on meter obliterates the charm of diversity, and can make any music monotonous. And alas, every bar-line suggests to the eye of the unintelligent player an accent, while there is nothing but his musical sense to suggest to him the far more important rhythmic accents. When we suffer from the metrical conscientiousness of the typical school-girl, mercilessly literalising some lovely fancy like Mozart's Minuet from the G-minor Symphony, how we wish that musical notation permitted us to

indicate rhythm as well as meter and to write
like this:

Figure XII

Thus notated, the passage may be played
with a literal observance of each bar-line without distortion, but in its original form the meas-
ure-accents must be suppressed in favor of the
phrase-accents.

"In the seventeenth century," observes
d'Indy in his *Cours de composition musicale,*
"the bar-line ceased to be merely a graphic sign;
it became a periodic starting point for the
rhythm, which it soon robbed of all its liberty
and elegance. Hence come those symmetrical
and square-cut forms to which we owe a great

179

part of the platitudes of the Italianism of the eighteenth and nineteenth centuries."

And again: "To beat the time and to give the rhythm of a musical phrase, are two completely distinct operations, often opposed. The coincidence of the rhythm and the measure is an entirely particular case, which men have unfortunately tried to generalise, propagating the error that 'the first beat of the measure is always strong.' This identification of rhythm with measure has had the most deplorable consequences for music. . . . Rhythm, submitted to the restricting requirements of meter, becomes rapidly impoverished, even to the most desolating platitude, just as a branch of a tree, strongly compressed by a ligature, becomes enfeebled and atrophied, while its neighbors absorb all the sap."

IV

So deplorable has become this abuse of mechanically regular metrical accent, especially in popular music, touching the unendurable in the deadly monotony of jazz, that we can understand how it should produce a strong reaction against all meter, such as we have recently witnessed in composers of the most various and conflicting schools. Stravinsky, in changing the time-signature in nearly every bar, is evidently compromising with the tyranny of the bar-line, accepting the vicious habit of an accent after every bar, but hoping to avoid monotony by changing the contents of every measure. Cyril Scott changes the time-signature nearly as often, but apparently with a more general object of merely baffling and eliminating the metrical sense. Others omit both time-signatures and bar-lines altogether. Still others recommend adopting the methods of earlier periods before bar-lines existed, such as that of the Gregorian chant. But aside from the fact that it is never possible in art to turn back the clock in this way, the matter is not so simple as all that. Meter is a Gordian knot that may be unravelled but cannot be cut. Music cannot now dispense with it, but must control it.

For see what happens when we try to eliminate meter. Suppose, for example, in the case of the opening of the Beethoven Fifth Symphony shown in Figure XI, accepting the conclusion reached above that "to accent the beginning of each measure is to make the passage . . . essentially unrhythmical," and that the most important points are those where there

are three, four, or five superposed accents, we
should jump to the conclusion that the merely
metrical accents (the two lower lines) were to
be entirely deleted. We should immediately
render the music unintelligible. Omit merely
the very first metrical accent shown, the one on
the second eighth-note, and its meaning is seriously jeopardised. Who has not heard it
played without that accent by careless conductors, and who has not then taken the first three
notes for a triplet, and in so doing lost the
whole force and energy of Beethoven's incomparable thought? Or take a somewhat similar
place in the Scherzo of the same composer's
"Harp" Quartet, opus 74, where all four instruments play in unison the vigorous rhythm:

Figure XIII

As any good quartet player will tell you, this
is a peculiarly difficult passage to make clear,
because the natural attack of the bows on the
three short notes tends to make an accent on
the first, which immediately turns the energetic

3-4 time into a vapid and obvious 6-8. As all
the instruments are playing the same thing
there is no way of bringing out the correct
meter except by consciously accenting the second instead of the first note of each group of
three. Then the musical meaning and value
at once return. Yet this accent is a purely
metrical one.

But we may go a step farther, and say that
metrical accents are not only oftentimes crucial
to musical meaning, but that they are often
essential to the larger rhythmic patterns with
which their careless use so interferes. A young
composer wrote a scherzo beginning with a
spirited rhythm for solo horn:

Figure XIV

Very well: a good idea. But the more experienced conductor pointed out to him that his
good idea would never reach his audience, because having nothing to guide them but their
ears they would naturally assume his theme
to be

Figure XV

the sorriest kind of a platitude. But what to do? Again the conductor had a suggestion. Simply put one kettle-drum stroke on that empty first beat, and the whole passage will fall into shape, the vigorous syncopation of the F and the long E getting its full value. Here the whole higher value of the rhythm is dependent on the index accent for the meter given by the drum. What a pity that Schumann did not have such a conductor at hand when he wrote his Manfred Overture! It begins with three syncopated chords, immensely exciting to any-one who knows they are syncopated. But no one knows it unless he either knows the music beforehand or watches the conductor's beat. Schumann's chords are shown at Figure XVI, A; the way they sound to the uninstructed lis-tener is noted at B. In this case there is no happy kettle-drum stroke tc give the rhythm its necessary metrical background.

Figure XVI

V

Metrical background:—it may be suggested in conclusion that that is what meter essentially is, the background necessary to the intelligibility of the rhythm; and that if it be either allowed to usurp the foreground, or on the other hand to fall entirely out of the picture, the meaning and beauty of the music are ruined. It is even through a certain more or less pronounced opposition between meter and rhythm that the most powerful and fascinating effects of music are often made; and for that opposition to make itself felt, the meter must evidently be present, but in the background. Suppose we play Dvořák's Slavonic Dance in C (Figure XVII, A) as the orchestra of a certain Swiss Kursaal plays it, omitting the metrical accents, in the evenly numbered measures, necessary to make clear the syncopations.

Figure XVII

At once it falls out of the amusingly syncopated 3-4 time into a pedestrian, painfully obvious 3-2 (Figure XVII, B) without any syncopations at all—or anything else of much interest. We have here an illuminating instance of the subtle relations with harmony often involved in effects that may at first sight seem purely rhythmical. A good deal of Dvořák's humor depends on the way he bobs away from the chord on the first beat (metrically accented) of each syncopated measure, and then with the rhythmically accented half-note bobs back again: so that we have harmony, meter, and

186

rhythm all playing battledore and shuttlecock together. In the 3-2 Kursaal version each measure remains monotonously and stupidly on one chord. This example, it will be noted, is just the opposite of the one from "My Country, 'tis of Thee." Here it is the 3-2 meter which is trite, the 3-4 which is piquant and alive.

As a general principle it will be found that wherever there are subtle syncopations or other rhythmic irregularities, their effect will depend on making the regular meter particularly clear upon their first appearance. After the cue has once been given, the ear of the hearer may to some extent be depended upon to hold it (within reason), and the metrical accents will therefore be subordinated to the rhythmical in order to avoid stiffness. For example, if in the Dvořák the metrical accents of the second and fourth measures are strongly indicated the hearer will catch the rhythm, and it will be unnecessary and undesirable to give them such prominence in later similar bars. The adjustment of the claims of meter and rhythm is one of the most delicate and revealing tasks with which every artist is tested. Overemphasise the meter, and your playing is prosaic, monotonous, and boresome; underemphasise it, and it is vague, vapid, and even more boresome. If you begin Schumann's lovely "Des Abends" without a gentle emphasis on the eighth notes in the left hand, to show us that the time is duple and that the triple movement of the melody is "against" it, you are no artist and give us no thrill of pleasure; but if you continue to stress your second beat a single measure after we have caught the idea and begun to play meter and rhythm against each other in our minds as a juggler keeps oranges in the air, then you are worse than no artist, you are a bungler. For meter must be servant, not tyrant; yet without meter rhythm cannot exist, and without a little wholesome opposition between them it cannot grow strong.

"Words in themselves," a shrewd critic has said, "are weak things, and even poetry does not get its effects by words; it does so by the action of words against the rhythm." [1] As with words, so it is with tones; music, like poetry, gets its effects by the action and reaction of rhythm (as embodied in motives) and meter; and that music is the most thrilling in

[1] Archibald Y. Campbell, on "Uses and Beauties of Plain Verse," London *Mercury*, April, 1925.

which these effects are the most potent, the most ingenious, and at the same time the most spontaneous and inevitable.

A NOTE ON ENGLISH RHYTHMS

D R. RALPH VAUGHAN WILLIAMS once dropped the suggestion, in a private conversation, that the supreme masters in the treatment of English texts were Purcell, Sir Arthur Sullivan, and the early madrigalists. Dr. Vaughan Williams is entitled to an opinion. His cycle of songs for tenor, string quartet, and piano, "On Wenlock Edge," based on the incomparable lyrics of A. E. Housman's "A Shropshire Lad," is certainly one of the finest modern examples of song-writing, and one of the finest examples from any period of song writing to texts in English. It is a striking example of the truth of the generalisation made by Deems Taylor in a newspaper article some years before he wrote the first practically successful American opera—"The King's Henchman"—that English sentences "depend upon accent for intelligibility," and must therefore be declaimed at the natural speed of speaking. Vaughan Williams would agree to this. "It is a mistake," he said in the conversation just mentioned, "to suppose that English is not spoken as rapidly as French or Italian. What makes these languages sound queer to us is their lack of accent. English syllables really go faster." Should not this fact of the rapidity of tempo of spoken English be constantly present to the minds of those who aspire to turn it into songs? Is not the neglect of it a frequent, perhaps the most frequent, cause of unintelligibility?

English phrases, it needs little introspection to realise, are habitually heard by us in groups, each with its characteristic rhythmic profile. The intelligibility of such groups is far less menaced by phonetic carelessness as to the purity of vowel sounds or even by slovenliness in the utterance of terminal consonants, such as we are constantly warned against by writers on opera in English, than by rhythmic deformation of them by the slowing up of subordinate syllables, about which little is written. When someone says to us, for example, an everyday phrase like "Good morning," especially if we are in a place—say the subway—where there are distracting noises, we recognise it far more by its rhythm than by its sounds. If the second syllable has the right predominance in length (and of course in pitch) over the subordinate first and third, we "get" the words whether we hear all the sounds or not. But if the short syllables be unduly lengthened, the most perfect clarity and accuracy in the mere sounds will not counteract such distortion. We shall not understand. Now in a song distracting noises are going on most of the time—the accompaniment. Truth to rhythmic patterns is therefore vital to intelligibility; and such truth requires not only adequate accent on the important syllables but, more in English than in other languages, adequate speed on the unimportant ones. Only the coöperation of these two technical means can achieve that peculiar kind of utterance that English requires, at once rapid and carefully graduated.

English is then, it should be clearly realised, peculiarly unfavorable to that sort of hand-to-mouth or word to word setting beloved of composers who, lacking lyric sweep and beauty, try to make up for it by descriptive expatiation on every idea or image suggested by the text. We have all heard, for our sins, those composers for whom a song is a sort of personally conducted sight-seeing trip and themselves the self-constituted guides who bawl at us through a megaphone what we are to observe. If a bird is mentioned by the poet, they cannot resist putting in a roulade in the treble; if a cannon, they must pound the bass.

There is a setting of "In Flanders Field," by an American composer, which is a perfect horror of this sort of literalism—a sort of complete guide-book to natural history, or musical "zoo." Such holding-up of the movement in order to pick out details is abhorrent to all real artists, who know by instinct that in any good song the whole is far more than the sum of the parts. It is even more abhorrent in dealing with English words than with French and German. Obviously, English words must be seized in handfuls, as they live in the phrases, rather than picked out like dead specimens with nippers; obviously they must rattle off with something of the clipped effect of ordinary speech, yet somehow be balanced and modulated into music too. It is the great difficulty of reconciling these conflicting necessities that makes the perfect setting of English so rare.

One of the greatest masters of this art was Sir Arthur Sullivan. Fortunately we have detailed information as to his method in **Law-**

rence's book about him; it is, as we should
have guessed from its results, the exact opposite of that of the word-setters. Sullivan
worked not from words but from phrases,
whole sentences, or even larger segments of
complete texts. Trying to grasp these large
units as wholes, he sought, to begin with, before considering melody at all, that rhythm of
all possible ones which would achieve a maximum of fluency, graceful movement, just emphasis on salient words, and distinctiveness or
charm. When by a patient application of the
trial and error method he had found that one
best rhythm, then and only then did he pass
to minor considerations such as pitch, melody,
harmony, dynamics and tone-color.

Lawrence gives an illuminating example in
the eight rhythms that Sullivan sketched for
the lines:

> "Were I thy bride,
> Then all the world beside
> Were not too wide
> To hold my wealth of love,
> Were I thy bride"

Figure XVIII

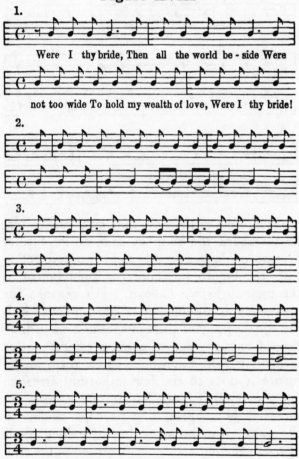

Of the eight rhythms that occurred to him he discarded the sixth as soon as its futility became evident; the others he worked out in full; the eighth he chose for embodiment in the melody as we have it. His reasons for preferring it to the others are obvious: it is the equal of any of them in speed, in subordination of unimportant syllables, a capital matter in dealing with English; it excels them in the justice it does to the few important stresses; and above all it has a fine formal balance, an indescribable charm, due perhaps chiefly to the parallelism between the three long notes at the beginning and their repetition at the end.

In short, it has the symmetry of music as well as the naturalness of speech.

Dr. Vaughan Williams modestly considers his own settings of Housman's verses not so good as those of his friend George Butterworth, whose death in the world war was a great loss to English music. Butterworth certainly shows an extraordinary blend of subtlety and simplicity in working out a seemingly inevitable rhythmic pattern for a complex piece of verse. Take, for instance, the following lines:

"The lads in their hundreds to Ludlow come in for
    the fair,
  There's men from the barn and the forge and the
    mill and the fold,
The lads for the girls and the lads for the liquor
    are there,
  And there with the rest are the lads that will never
    be old."

How is one to set music to a text such as that? The first problem is to find a general pattern, subject to local modifications as they may be needed, which shall reproduce, in musical terms, something of the flow, the speed, the jaunty narrative ease of the words. Anyone who will glance at Figure XIX will concede that Butterworth has solved it.

Figure XIX

forge and the mill and the fold.

The mixture of 6-8 and 9-8 time, or more accurately speaking, of measures of two and three main divisions, or "large beats," respectively, is ingenious to a degree and yet so natural that only an analyst will realise that it is the balancing of 2 and 3 (or 5) of these large beats with 2 and 4 (or 6) that gives the couplet its charm, its indescribable sense of rightness, and raises it from "patter" to music.

But the solution of this problem of design alone is not enough, as we see if we imagine the same design applied again to the second couplet, as an inferior composer might apply it. There would result a lack of flexibility, a sense of mechanical formula, applied by rote, fatal to beauty. Something more is needed

Figure XX

than even the very charming irregularity of balance already achieved, of five against six. That irregularity was evidently dictated by almost purely musical considerations to give a moment of poise on the word "fold," for there is no expressive or dramatic need to differentiate "fold" from the equally important "barn," "forge" and "mill." But in the second couplet we meet another problem which calls for a different solution: how to meet the needs of expression by dwelling on certain words—to put more "feeling," as we say, into the utterance, yet without checking the naturalness of the flow. Figure XX shows how Butterworth solves this second and more difficult problem.

The melody, and especially the harmony, are so modified that we get the two additional poises on "the rest" and "lads," while the irregular balance is rendered even more fascinating by the scheme of 5 and 7 as answer to the former 5 and 6.

It is hardly too much to say that the necessity for combining rapid movement naturally accentuated with the flexibility required both by formal beauty and by expression makes the setting of English texts one of the greatest feats of technical virtuosity that can be required of a composer. Well does Ernest Newman say in a remarkable paper on this subject in the London *Musical Times* (Volume 59, page 395): "Thousands of [German] verses fall naturally into familiar musical meters, but it is impossible to confine within such simple fixed meters a variable, fluid, organic thing like this lyric of Shakespeare's:

> " 'Come away, come away, death,
>   And in sad cypress let me be laid.'

"Even to this day no English composer has succeeded in finding the veritable rhythmical equivalent in music of these lines of Shake-speare."

One wonders what would be Newman's judgment of this setting of the lines by the Italian composer, Mario Castelnuovo Tedesco.

Figure XXI

It certainly has a rare beauty, even if it does not, as it proceeds, entirely escape monotony, or achieve that combination of natural flow and expressive emphasis that is so remarkable in the best work of Butterworth.

CREATIVE LEISURE

I

A PARADOX of our modern world that grows no less exasperating with increasing familiarity is that the greater the amount of leisure that science, applied in industry, puts at our disposal, the more unleisurely, hurried, distracted, noisy, and feverish our actual life seems to become. Writers like Kropotkin, Lord Leverhulme, Wells, Russell, show us how, with modern industrial methods, we could with seven, six, or even five hours' work a day for each of us, produce all the goods we need for all; yet this magical liberation from the curse of work, undreamed of by our ancestors, we are wholly unable to use in such wise as to make our lives more noble, deliberate, refined and beautiful. We are defeated in all our efforts to make a fine use of these new and glorious possibilities—defeated, not alone by a stupid economic inertia that perpetuates ancient outworn privileges and abuses, but even more helplessly by the far more intractable because

deeper-lying psychological stupidity that pre-
vents us from knowing, even when we get it,
what we want to do with our leisure. As always happens to intelligence when it is not alert
enough to dominate material developments for
its own ends, they dominate it. Even more
than in Emerson's day, "Things are in the
saddle, and ride mankind." Our very novel-
ists weary and depress us with their descrip-
tions of Babbitt and of the Main Street into
which he has turned our drab civilisation. All
the more serious sociological books devote
much of their attention to the ugliness,
monotony, and fatigue that industrialism, thus
abused, has brought into the world. One of
the most recent and most suggestive of such
books, M. André Siegfried's "America Comes
of Age," while pointing out that our "material
advance is immeasurable in comparison with the
Old World," rightly insists that "from the
point of view of individual refinement and art
the sacrifice is real indeed." "Even the
humblest European," he says, "sees in art an
aristocratic symbol of his own personality, and
modern America has no national art and does
not even feel the need of one." (Here he is
of course using the word art in the widest sense

possible, as a sort of symbol of all that is happy, free, and self-determined in human life.) "Many of the most magnificent material achievements of the United States," he continues, "have been made possible only by sacrificing certain rights of the individual, which we in the Old World regard as among the most precious victories of civilisation. . . . To America the advent of the new order is a cause for pride, but to Europe it brings heart-burnings and regrets for a state of society that is doomed to disappear."

It is not only Europeans that look with dismay on this inevitable disappearance of the old civilisation, doomed not only in America but in the whole world, plainly destined to become progressively Americanised. Thoughtful Americans too are painfully aware, as our literature shows, of this terrifying drabness that our machine-system is imposing on the world. The trouble with us is not that we do not think of it, but that we think of it too often sentimentally, in a mere vain hankering after old civilisations forever gone, or cynically and uncreatively, in the fashion of the popular denouncers and ridiculers. What we need is to think about it realistically and inventively: realistically, recognising how inevitable it is and no longer wasting our strength in futile efforts to evade it; inventively, discovering gradually by analysis and experiment how material prosperity, so vain in itself, can be transformed into the ultimate human values. M. Siegfried recognises that there is some effort among us at such constructive thought. "Having refused to save the individuality of the factory worker," he says, "[thoughtful Americans] shift their defence to other grounds. During the day the worker may be only a cog in the machine, they say; but in the evening at any rate he becomes a man once more. His leisure, his money, the very things which mass production puts at his disposal, these will restore to him the manhood and intellectual independence of which his highly organised work has deprived him."

With this may be compared the following passage in "The Prospects of Industrial Civilisation," by Bertrand and Dora Russell: "A great deal less work is required now to produce a given amount of goods than was required before the industrial revolution, and yet people live at higher pressure than they did then. . . . The whole urgency of the modern business world is toward speeding up, greater efficiency, more intense international competition, when it ought to be toward more ease, less hurry, and combination to produce goods for use rather than for profit. The important progress now is not in industrial production but in ideas."

There is thus considerable recognition that it is idle to combat directly the spread of industrialism and the mechanisation of the worker it inevitably brings about. A more hopeful attack is to start with the increasing amount of leisure time made possible by industrialism itself (at least if it could be combined with an enlightened social system) and see whether the values lost might not be there restored. Such an attempt can be successful, however, only with the aid of an understanding of the psychological peculiarities that determine our enjoyment and use of leisure. Our first questions must accordingly be: "What precisely do we mean by leisure?—and under what conditions can it be fruitful?"

II

Perhaps in thinking out our answers to these questions it will be helpful first of all to recognise candidly that at present, among us in

America, little true leisure exists—what we have is mostly not the genuine article. We have plenty of what we carelessly suppose to be leisure—more, probably, thanks to our economic good fortune, than is to be found anywhere else in the world; but most of it, spoiled by wrong emotional attitudes and fallacious ideas, falls short of creativeness, and so is not real leisure at all. The wrong attitudes and ideas which spoil it are largely, as might be expected, by-products of industrialism. Perhaps the most insidious one is the jaded emotional state, seldom consciously recognised, that results from industrial monotony and denial of personal initiative. The fatigue-poisoned mind and body, too dull to enjoy quiet beauty and true thought, crave the crude excitements so abused among us: restless speeding in motor-cars from nowhere to nowhere; the rapid movements and trivial but exciting physical dangers of the amusement park; superlatives and exaggerations in talk; the artificial stimulants and feverish pumped-up gaiety of the "wild party"; the "thrills" so insistently demanded by the younger generation; violent plastic arts using harsh angles and garish colors; noisy, mechanical, over-accented music. The "jazz age" in a word is a jaded and joyless age, incapable of the happy serenity of creative leisure.

And this pervasive emotional attitude is unfortunately reënforced by a pervasive fallacious idea, also derived largely from industrialism. Because quantity production works well in the manufacture of shoes (at least well so far as concerns the cheap production of a great many shoes of a sort), we assume too uncritically that it can be applied to more vital matters, and that we can play as well as work in herds. We all go to the same "shows," listen to the same tunes broadcast from the same stations, sight-see the same sights from the same char-à-bancs, even read the same books chosen for us by the same witch-doctors. We accept, in fact, a regimentation of our leisure, blissfully unconscious of the ironic absurdity of such a process. Hence in general, and by and large, what ought to be leisure in America is joyless and feverish instead of joyful and creative, and gregarious and regimented rather than individual and full of personal initiative. It is a killing of time instead of a time for living.

It ought to be self-evident, however, that a feverishly empty and mechanically regimented leisure can be no corrective for monotonous and rigidly organised industrialism; and that if what we are seeking is something to supply the sense of satisfying activity and of individual self-realisation that the mediæval craftsman got, and that the fortunately situated modern artist or man of science can still get, from work, we must somehow arrive at a quite different sense and conception of leisure. One way to arrive at it is to recognise that the conditions of creative leisure must be after all very similar to those of creative work; that if work had not been mechanised and regimented by industrialism, we should have no problem of leisure, since everyone would get his instinctive satisfactions through his work; and that, as things are, the essential matter is to find out by what means leisure can be made to give as much as possible of these instinctive satisfactions to the majority of men and women who have been unhappily but irremediably deprived of them in their work by modern conditions. Except for a small, exceptionally situated minority, our contemporaries spend their lives in an alternation between a work that because of its monotony, or its imposition by others, or both, gives them little or no sense of self-expression and social contribution, and an idleness that is equally empty and vain. Surely in such a world it is a matter of vital importance to ask to what extent and by what means not only the factory workers and the vast army of clerks, but all of us caught in the industrial machine, can get in our spare hours, fortunately increasing in number, that sense of fruitful life which comes in supreme degree to workers like the mediæval craftsman and the modern artist and man of science.

III

The analogy between creative work and creative leisure comes out strikingly in the fact that both require a peculiar kind of discipline— a discipline imposed not by outer authority but by oneself. The younger generation, in the natural reaction from submission to authority with which most open-minded older people heartily sympathise, has suffered severely here by confusing discipline with authority and rejecting the one with the other, thus rendering its leisure uncreative and unsatisfying. A large part of its demand for "thrills" is sheer dissatisfaction and a puzzled sense of somehow having been cheated out of the charm of life. The remedy is to analyse anew the conception of discipline, separating it completely from its unfortunate and misleading associations with authority, basing it on a scientifically realistic psychology. We are obliged to value discipline not because it is moral, or respectable, or commended by anyone, but because through it we can get the satisfactions we crave, while without it we cannot. It is true that at the threshold of this analysis we meet a familiar theoretical difficulty. To most people the ideas of leisure and of discipline are mutually exclusive. They can hardly admit that leisure can be disciplined and remain leisure. A disciplined leisure seems to them as great an absurdity as a regimented leisure. Does leisure that submits to discipline, they ask, remain truly leisure at all? This is, no doubt, the central irreducible problem of our whole investigation. Were it not for the apparent theoretical opposition between leisure and discipline, and the equally unescapable practical necessity of combining them in our experience, the whole problem of leisure would be simpler than it is.

Let us begin, however, with what all will probably agree to: namely, that there is in fruitful leisure a certain attitude at first sight indifferent to discipline, if not actually opposed

to it, which we may call spontaneity, or even irresponsibility. This is one of its most universally acknowledged elements, and undoubtedly
one of its most precious ones. It is akin to what
Bliss Perry has called "The Amateur Spirit,"
and in the book of that name illustrates in the
saying of a Williams professor: "If you are
turning a grindstone, every moment is precious;
but if you are doing a man's work, the inspired
moments are precious." It is celebrated by
Stevenson in his delightful "Apology for
Idlers" and typified in Sainte-Beuve, who, he
says, "as he grew older, came to regard all
experience as one great book, in which to study
for a few years ere we go hence; and it seemed
all one to him whether you should read in Chapter XX, which is the differential calculus, or
in Chapter XXXIX, which is hearing the band
play in the gardens." Its sanative value to
those who, like most Americans, are over-regi-
mented, and therefore over-tense, is suggested
in this wise advice of Dr. G. E. Partridge:
"Teach the mind to fall apart like the body in
relaxation, by letting it lapse into revery. Cultivate the habit of complete idleness. Doing
nothing is often the best use of time. Even
ideas sprout in such a medium. Little things

leak into the soul worth inviting. The mind may be accustomed, in its spare moments, to become de-individuated, to live the life of the universal, and thus to gain power for its own ends." All these observers emphasise the spontaneous element in leisure, which even when not creative is at least highly re-creative: its evasion of routine and of the rigidifying effect of habit, its wholesome surrender to free-ranging curiosity. Inspired moments are such moments of spontaneous interest[1] freed from routine preoccupations and conventional standards, in which the individual throws off his harness and goes, so to speak, "out to grass."

And together with his harness, Pegasus throws off all thought of cab-fare. Leisure, that is to say, is not only spontaneous, in that its creative preoccupation with the new, the tentative, the experimental, obliges it to escape from routine, from all that is set, fixed, completed, but also irresponsible, in that the experimental values just feeling their way into being are obliged to avoid already recognised values, especially practical and financial values. Leisure is profoundly unutilitarian. Whatever else

[1] For further examples see the present writer's "Artistic Ideals," the essay on "Spontaneity."

it may or may not be made to do, it can never, thank God, be made to "pay." It is by its deepest nature discovering and enjoying truths whose future use (should they prove to have any) depends on their present uselessness. The Russells give a good example of this. "Mendelism," they point out, "is now studied by hosts of agriculturists and stock-breeders, but Mendel was a monk, who spent his leisure enjoying his peas blossoms. A million years of practical agriculturists would never have discovered Mendelism. . . . The utilitarianism of commercial industry must ultimately kill the pure desire for knowledge, just as it kills the very analogous artistic impulse. In America, where the more utilitarian aspects of science are keenly appreciated, no great advance in pure theory has been made."

IV

But however spontaneous and irresponsible leisure may be, we are never allowed to forget that capricious it is not. This we all learn sooner or later, to our sorrow, from personal experience. In a time of strenuous work, for example, we dream of what we shall do, or of how gloriously we shall do nothing, in our next holidays. Then at last, we promise ourselves, we shall be at no man's beck and call, we shall submit to no rules, we shall follow our own sweet will. But when at length the holidays arrive, we find to our dismay that our own sweet will is not sweet at all, but sour and bitter, and leaves a bad taste in our mouths. For if before we were the servants of a social situation, now we are the slaves of our own caprices, which is far worse. We are like ships without rudders. One day, in a mood of self-indulgence, we eat too much, drink too much, smoke too much; the next, in an equally futile reaction of asceticism, we impose meaningless and irritating penances on ourselves; no day is satisfying, because none has continuity with others, none brings us the sense of power, control, and tranquillity we need in order to be happy.

It is obvious, then, that leisure, in order to be fruitful and to make us happy, needs some such stimulus and control as work gets largely through social means; and our next question must therefore be, how can these be achieved in the case of leisure without jeopardising, as direct social control would seem to do, its equally essential spontaneity and irresponsibility? This brings us back to our fundamental problem of how leisure can be compatible with discipline, since it is evidently a kind of discipline that we need here.

We may first observe that the moments of inspiration no more make up the whole of creative leisure than of creative work. Actually, as we know by experience, they are few and far between, separated by long intervals in which we hope for them in vain. What is going on in these intervals? In the masterly analysis contained in his book "The Art of Thought," Graham Wallas divides the whole creative process into four stages, preparation, incubation, inspiration, and verification, the first and last conscious, the others unconscious. Preparation he describes as a stage of "hard, conscious, systematic and fruitless analysis of the problem." Its function is to provide the mind with its materials, to charge the battery as it were, so that the spark of inspiration may later shoot vigorously. Poincaré, in his famous account of his way of making his mathematical discoveries in the book "Science and Method," agrees with Wallas as to the indispensability of the conscious stage of preparation. "Unconscious work," he says, "is not possible, or in any case not fruitful, unless it is first preceded and then followed by a period of conscious work. These sudden inspirations are never produced . . . except after some days of voluntary efforts which appeared absolutely fruitless, in which one thought one had accomplished nothing, and seemed to be on a totally wrong track. These efforts, however, were not as barren as one thought; they set the unconscious machine in motion, and without them it would not have worked at all, and would not have produced anything."

The long and laborious stage of conscious preparation is followed by an equally long or longer stage of unconscious incubation, almost more difficult to bear, because one is now working in the dark. A process of trial and error goes on, below the threshold of consciousness, in which the materials are ceaselessly shaped and reshaped, and all possible associations worked out with the freshness and amplitude made possible by the abeyance of the conscious will, and when a successful combination happens, it irrupts into consciousness as an "inspiration." Poincaré felt that in his own case it was his intense delight in the æsthetic beauty of a true solution that brought it into consciousness. With this Varendonck, who in his "The

Psychology of Day-dreams" reports the results of a long course of introspection, is in agreement. "Since I have accustomed myself to observe my unconscious life," he says, "I often become aware of the intellectual work which goes on piece-meal without the interference of my conscious faculties. But unless it evokes an emotion resembling the joy of discovery, I do not interrupt it." And again: "We become aware only when the right solution is hit upon beyond the threshold, and thanks to our ignorance of all the previous attempts we obtain the idea of a rapidity which does not correspond with the reality." Similarly Poincaré sees in the "appearances of sudden illumination" we call inspirations, "obvious indications of a long course of previous unconscious work." "Often," he says, "when a man is working at a difficult problem, he accomplishes nothing the first time he sets to work. Then he takes more or less of a rest, and sits down again at his table. During the first half-hour he still finds nothing, and then all at once the decisive idea presents itself to his mind. . . . The rest was occupied with unconscious work, and the result of this work was afterwards revealed . . . during a period of conscious work, but independently of that work, which at most only performs the unlocking process, as if it were the spur that excited into conscious form the results already acquired during rest, which till then remained unconscious."

In the light of these analyses, we realise that just as the part of an iceberg we see shining so brilliantly in the sun is but an insignificant fragment of the vast bulk that under water is hidden from our vision, so the moments of inspiration, for all their charm, play a small part in the creative process in comparison with the laborious efforts that consciously prepare and unconsciously incubate them. If we wish to make our leisure creative it is necessary that we recognise to the full the laboriousness of these its preliminary processes. Preparation, as both Wallas and Poincaré remark, is essentially full of fruitless effort,—and what requires more courage and more patience than to continue efforts one knows to be fruitless? And incubation is a series of trials in which the errors greatly outnumber the successes. "Fertility of imagination," as Jevons puts it, "and abundance of guesses at truth are among the first requisites of discovery; but the erroneous guesses must be many times as numerous as those which prove well-founded." "The world little knows," remarks Faraday, "how many of the thoughts and theories that have passed through the mind of a scientific investigator have been crushed in silence and secrecy by his own severe criticism and adverse examination; that in the most successful instances not a tenth of the suggestions, the hopes, the wishes, the preliminary conclusions, have been re-alised."

V

In a process so arduous as creativeness is thus shown to be, it is evident enough that the individual must have all the social support he can possibly get—without it he could hardly hope to find the courage for such a long fruit-lessness of effort, the patience for so heart-breaking a fumbling in the dark of trial and error. Yet this support must not impede his spontaneity nor regiment his irresponsibility. This is our final problem. The answer to it appears to point to more loose and subtle social groupings than those definitely organised ones that serve as a background for work. We seem to be developing nowadays new techniques for

all sorts of informal groups—groups for amateur theatricals, for choruses, for athletic
games, for debates and intellectual discussions
—that bring social stimulus to the aid of individual initiative without hampering it. Still
freer are those spontaneous companionships
and friendships that are always springing up in
colleges, and that often do far more for the
development of those who participate in them
than more formal education. And then there
are the comradeships of scientific men and artists of which their biographies and correspondence are so inspiringly full: Darwin and
Huxley, fighting shoulder to shoulder the superstitions of their day; Flaubert and George
Sand, or Stevenson and Henry James, discussing the function of literature; Brahms and
Joachim exchanging exercises in counterpoint;
Curie and Madame Curie delighting the world
with the spectacle of a marriage of true minds.
In all such associations there is a maximum of
stimulus with a minimum of inhibition that is
full of suggestion for our gregarious and overregimented America. The English have a better instinct for how free individuals may cooperate; the English leisure class have already
developed traditions of sportsmanship, of

noblesse oblige, which make their leisure more fruitful than ours, so that it may in the future serve the world as a sort of rough sketch of what enlightened leisure may become.

Finally, there is that subtlest form of social stimulus which inheres in the individual's awareness of a common body of knowledge, such as the psychological laws of creativeness at which we have been glancing. It is quite possible that some day, as psychological knowledge becomes widespread, everyone will be expected to make some valid contribution to society with his leisure, and that it will be thought disgraceful to kill time in mere pastimes or stagnant ennui, and we shall be ashamed to be bored.

As understanding spreads of the way in which creativeness functions, each individual will at once be stimulated to undertake some worthy development of his peculiar powers, and safeguarded not only against mere frittering but also against the stagnation of intellectual pride and the fixations of those who love success better than discovery. After one of the informal discussions that follow Dr. H. A. Overstreet's lectures on psychology, a student wrote him a letter which he prints in the appendix to his book "Influencing Human Behaviour." "We must fumble," wrote this student, "and by chance we may make a success. If we do, we shall have the creative intelligence. . . . Perhaps the difference between those with and those without creative intelligence consists in this: those with it try to do something they can't (yet) do; and the others have the fixation that one has to learn to do something first, otherwise there is no use trying to do it. . . . Perhaps the words artist, poet, writer, musician, inventor and so on are evil stereotypes, preventing people from trying to do what artists, writers, poets, do. The stereotype we all need is the idea embodied in the statement 'function makes faculty.' This statement should be rewritten in terms of modern psychology, in forms that will stick."

The way to creative leisure would thus seem to lie through a widely-shared understanding of such fundamental psychological truths as these, affording us all, as individuals, a social stimulus sufficient to carry us through the strenuous preparatory and incubatory stages of creativeness, yet not depriving us, as all regimentation and organisation cannot but do, of the spontaneity and irresponsibility equally essential.

And it is well to remember that the path to creative leisure is also the path to the highest and deepest joys of which we are capable.

THE PARADOX OF BEETHOVEN

I

THE appearance in 1920 of Thayer's "Life of Beethoven" marked the happy but long delayed conclusion of a curious literary episode. The work, though recognised as authoritative ever since its publication in German, had had to wait over half a century for publication in the language of its American author, Alexander W. Thayer. That an American should have been able to produce, in the middle of the nineteenth century when our musical life was so primitive, the standard biography of the great German composer, is in itself noteworthy. But that this book should never have been completed by him, that he should never have been paid a dollar for what gradually became the chief work of his life, and that it should not have appeared in English until nearly twenty-five years after his death—all this is not only strange, but to Americans of musical feeling a matter for uncomfortably mingled pride and humiliation.

Alexander Wheelock Thayer, born in 1817 and graduated at Harvard in 1843, made in two visits to Europe in 1849-51 and 1854-56 such valuable researches in the life of Beethoven that Dr. Lowell Mason and Mrs. Mehetabel Adams gave him financial help towards establishing himself permanently abroad. He later supported himself by entering the consular service, living for many years at Trieste, devoting all his leisure to his beloved study, facilitated by such remarkable tributes to its value as the sending to Trieste by the Royal Library of Berlin of the Conversation Books used by Beethoven in the years of his deafness. The first volume of the biography, translated into German and edited by Dr. Hermann Deiters, appeared in 1866; the second in 1872; the third in 1879. Then Thayer's health failed. He gave up his post in 1882 "because," as he said, "of utter inability longer to continue Beethoven work and official labor together." Even so he could not command the strength needed.

"I am now compelled," he wrote to Sir George Grove in 1895, "to relinquish all hope of ever being able to do the work. There are

two great difficulties to be overcome : the one is
that all the letters and citations are in the original German . . . ; the other, there is much to
be condensed. . . . I am continually in conflict
with all previous writers and was compelled,
therefore, to show in my text that I was right.
. . . Now the case is changed. A. W. T.'s
novelties are now, with few exceptions, accepted as facts and can, in the English edition,
be used as such. . . . I have no expectation of
ever receiving any pecuniary recompense for
my forty years of labor, for my years of poverty arising from the costs of my extensive
researches."

Thayer died in 1897. Meanwhile a revised
German edition of the biography, begun by
Deiters and continued after his death by Dr.
Hugo Riemann, was carried to completion, on
the basis of Thayer's papers, in 1911. By
1914 Henry E. Krehbiel, of the New York
Tribune, who had worked much with Thayer,
had completed an English text, based upon
the author's original manuscripts and this revised German edition, and had even written
an introduction for it, dated July, 1914. The
war postponed publication once more. Finally
in 1920, seventy-two years after Thayer began

his researches, his work was published in his own language, thanks to the financial assistance of the Beethoven Association of New York, a group of musicians giving their services without pay, and devoting to this high purpose the proceeds of their season of 1920-21. Such is the story of the strange vicissitudes of Thayer's "Beethoven."

The book is an admirable one. "I fight for no theories," said its author, "and cherish no prejudices; my sole point of view is the truth." It was no idle boast, nor was the point of view suggested an easy one of attainment in dealing with a life so idealised out of all likeness to reality by generations of sentimentalists. Thayer's method is the indefatigably minute collection of all the evidence. Mr. Krehbiel remarks in a note, for example. "Thayer made practically a complete transcript of the Conversation Books [of which Schindler had saved 138 out of the 400 left by Beethoven] laboriously deciphering the frequently hieroglyphic scrawls, and compiled a mass of supplementary material for the purpose of fixing the chronological order of the conversations. The dates of all concerts and other public events alluded to were established by the examination of newspapers and other contemporaneous records" . . .

He had the true scientist's preference for the pettiest fact to the most specious fancy, combined with inexhaustible patience in tracing every scrap of paper and unravelling every knot of error and misunderstanding; and his book thus becomes the permanent authoritative source for Beethoven's life. Its defects are trivial, when weighed against this supreme merit of impartiality and scientific realism. They are, first, that save for the professional investigator its pages are almost surcharged with details, most of them highly unimportant in isolation, and having for the casual reader little apparent bearing upon each other; second, that such attempts as are made to philosophise these findings, and to build up a theory of the strangely paradoxical character outlined, are based on a Victorian view of ethics and psychology, and leave many puzzles unresolved. This is the more to be regretted in that Beethoven would be an incomparable "case" for study by modern psycho-analytic methods.

Were such a study made, one feels after a careful reading of Thayer that it might take

as its point of departure the conception of
Beethoven as a man of innate nobility and gen-
erosity of character, constantly thwarted,
balked, and exasperated in all his dealings with
the world, and at last disastrously—so far as
his own happiness was concerned—thrown in
upon himself by a complete lack of social discipline. In paradoxical contrast with this external failure would appear the marvellous inner
success achieved by a self-imposed discipline in
music. One here conceives discipline, of course,
not as the imposition of any arbitrary external
authority—which Beethoven would have been
splendidly right in rejecting—but as a self-
sought technique for dealing with the world
about one, and consequently a prerequisite of
freedom. Not acquiring this, he was not free
but a slave, the slave of his own moods and
whims. There is something almost mad in his
subjection to his own high temper, even when
there is righteousness in his anger. Förster
relates that in 1802, not long after Beethoven
first came to Vienna to live, he was playing
with Förster, four hands, some marches of his
at the house of Count Browne. Young Count
Browne disturbed him by conversation with
a lady. "Beethoven, after several efforts had

vainly been made to secure quiet, suddenly took my hands from the keys in the middle of the music, jumped up, and said very loudly, 'I will not play for such swine!' "

As he grew older his fits of fury grew ever more unmanageable and more unreasonable, and were directed often against his closest friends. At a rehearsal of "Fidelio" in 1805, Prince Lobkowitz unwisely made light of the absence of the third bassoon. "This so enraged the composer," says Thayer, "that, as he passed the Lobkowitz place, on his way home, he could not restrain the impulse to turn aside and shout in at the great door of the palace, 'Lobkowitz ass!' " His regular epithet for his publishers was "hell-hounds," and he was especially fond of the phrase "hell-hounds who lick and gnaw my brains." The increasing deafness of his last years inflamed his suspiciousness of those most loyal to his interests until in 1824, after Lichnowsky, Schuppanzigh and Schindler had met at his rooms to arrange the first performance of the Ninth Symphony, he sent them the three famous notes:

To Lichnowsky: "I despise treachery. Do not visit me again. No concert."

To Schuppanzigh: "Let him [1] not visit me more. I shall give no concert."

To Schindler: "I request you not to come again until I send for you. No concert."

It is worthy of note that by this time the friends paid little attention to such outbursts. They proceeded with the arrangements for the concert, which was given with great artistic success. Beethoven, however, was dissatisfied with the financial returns. He gave a dinner to Schindler, Umlauf (who had conducted, Beethoven being now prevented from conducting by his deafness) and Schuppanzigh. "He had ordered an 'opulent' meal," says Thayer, "but no sooner had the party sat down to table than the 'explosion which was imminent' came. In the plainest terms he burst out with the charge that the management and Schindler had cheated him. Umlauf and Schuppanzigh tried to convince him that this was impossible . . . Beethoven persisted . . . Schindler and Umlauf left the room. Schuppanzigh remained behind just long enough to get a few stripes on his broad back and then joined his companions

[1] Beethoven habitually used the third person with Schuppanzigh.

235

in misery. Together they finished their meal at a restaurant in the Leopoldstadt."

Such irrational anger and lack of self-control is mad—or rather it is childish; and almost equally childish were the outbursts of exaggerated remorse with which Beethoven, especially in his younger years, often reacted against these fits of petulance. He writes to his friend Wegeler of Bonn days, for instance, in terms both ludicrous and pathetic: "Dearest! Best! In what an odious light you have exhibited me to myself! I acknowledge it, I do not deserve your friendship. . . . You think that I have lost some of my goodness of heart, but, thank Heaven! it was no intentional or deliberate malice which induced me to act as I did towards you; it was my inexcusable thoughtlessness which did not permit me to see the matter in its true light. O, how ashamed I am, not only for your sake but also for my own. O let me say for myself, I was always good, and always strove to be upright and true in my actions—otherwise, how could you have loved me? Could I have changed so fearfully for the worse in such a short time? Impossible: these feelings of goodness and love of righteousness cannot have died for ever in me

236

in a moment." And so on, at great length. Yet Beethoven is right: even through the turgid emotionalism of his sentences we feel an essentially noble heart, pathetically untrained, tragically at the mercy of its own fluctuating moods.

Indeed, how could we expect it to be otherwise when we study his early years? His childhood, the period of supreme importance, as Freud has shown, in the fixing of mental peculiarities, could hardly have been more unfavorable. His father, weak, dissipated, and greedy, incited by the brilliant career of Mozart as a boy prodigy, exploits him from very babyhood. "Cäcilia Fischer," quotes Thayer from Hennes, "still sees him, a tiny boy, standing on a footstool in front of the clavier," and "Herr Burgmaster Windeck . . . saw the little Louis van Beethoven standing in front of the clavier and weeping." On 26 March, 1778, the father announces that he will "have the honor to present his little son of six years [sic] who will contribute various clavier-concertos and trios." The composer was really seven years old in the preceding December. Thayer considers that the father falsified the age to enhance the éclat of the performance.

At about eleven "all other studies were abandoned in favor of music." At about the same period, often when Pfeiffer, his teacher, "came with Beethoven, the father, from the winehouse late at night, the boy was roused from sleep and kept at the pianoforte until morning." No wonder he was "a shy and taciturn boy, the necessary consequence of the life apart that he led, observing more and pondering more than he spoke, and disposed to abandon himself entirely to the feelings awakened by music and later by poetry and to the pictures created by fancy." His mother died when he was sixteen. Two years later the father's drunkenness obliged Beethoven, not yet quite nineteen, but the eldest of three brothers, to petition the elector to make him the responsible head of his family. About three years later still, the end of this unfortunate parent is commemorated in a casual sentence in a letter of the Elector-Archbishop of Bonn: "The revenues of the liquor-excise have suffered a loss in the deaths of Beethoven and Eichhoff."

The significance of all this is that Beethoven, as a high-strung boy, met at every turn by irrational severity or equally irrational indulgence —for we may guess that so foolish a father

238

must sometimes have "spoiled" so profitable a son—missed irretrievably the smooth functioning in his environment that, could he have achieved it, would have won him, thanks to his far more than ordinary intellectual powers, a rare measure of peace and happiness. Instead of this, he found himself ever more thwarted and balked, more and more cut off and thrown back on himself, more and more the victim of a sharp division in his world, his "me" standing trenchantly opposed to his milieu. For one naturally high-spirited and inclined to pride, this was a calamitous misfortune.

Anecdotes and letters of the middle period point to an almost insane inflammation of the "me" sense. Beethoven lived for some time in the house of his patron, Prince Lichnowsky. "The Prince," relates Wegeler, "once directed his serving man that if ever he and Beethoven should ring at the same time the latter was to be first served. Beethoven heard this, and the same day engaged a servant for himself. In the same manner, once when he took a whim to learn to ride, which speedily left him, the stable of the Prince being offered him, he bought a horse." A contemporary account of his rivalry with the pianist Wöelfl concludes:

"Wöelfl enjoys an advantage because of his amiable bearing, contrasted with the somewhat haughty pose of Beethoven." Haydn nicknamed him "The Great Mogul," and Frau von Barnhard tells of his "refusing to play, when Countess Thun, Prince Lichnowsky's mother, a very eccentric woman, had fallen on her knees before him as he lay on the sofa, to beg him to." We have another picture of Beethoven in these early Vienna days, in one of his own letters, often quoted. Describing a walk with Goethe when they were met by the entire Imperial family, he remarks: "Goethe withdrew his arm from mine, in order to stand aside. . . . I pressed down my hat more firmly on my head, buttoned up my greatcoat, and, crossing my arms behind me, I made my way through the thickest portion of the crowd. Princes and courtiers formed a line for me; Archduke Rudolph took off his hat and the Empress bowed to me first."—and this rather absurdly boyish account ends with the boast "These great ones of the earth *know me.*"—Beethoven's own italics. Prince Lobkowitz once reminded him, when he had been saying that he ought not to have to bargain with his publishers, as Goethe and Handel did not bargain with theirs, that he had not as yet their authority and reputation. He replied: "With men who will not believe and trust in me because I am as yet unknown to universal fame, I can not hold intercourse!"

Here Beethoven appears certainly not devoid of a lovable high spirit, a kind of rough nobility, but dangerously undisciplined, ominously unable to communicate on equal terms with others. His statement regarding his friends in a letter of about this time: "I value them only by what they do for me. . . . I look upon them only as instruments upon which I play when I feel so disposed," though it doubtless must not be taken too literally, is rightly regarded by Thayer with consternation, and may be compared with this Nietzschean pronouncement: "I want none of your moral precepts, for power is the morality of men who loom above the others." Never having been trained to see things from other angles than his own, and being gradually more and more cut off from intercourse by his deafness and his absorption in his work, he finally became quite isolated and helpless, unable to manage any social situation, a comical and sometimes a tragic victim of that strange outer world that he yearned towards but could not grasp. So far as his social relations went, his life was aborted at every turn by his complete lack of the technique that only discipline could have won him. In his music alone are revealed the priceless treasures of nobility and tenderness hidden beneath that repellant mask.

II

It was the paradox of Beethoven's nature, then, that the extraordinary success he achieved in his music, through learning from earliest youth to deal skilfully with its material, was in no wise matched in any of the affairs of daily life, which on the contrary he systematically botched because he had never learned to deal with them. This failure to function efficiently in social relations threw him back upon himself, developed in him a pathological sense of opposition between himself and others, and established a vicious circle by which the more he mishandled them the more alien they came to seem to him, and the more alien they seemed the less did he attempt a deeper understanding and sympathy that might have straightened things out. Of course, the supreme instance was the tragedy of his relations with his nephew Karl, for whose attempt at suicide he was undoubtedly somewhat responsible through his unwise mingling of severity and indulgence; the story may be read in all its pathos and irony in Thayer's third volume.

In smaller matters and less intimate relations his utter and complacent unawareness of other personalities is often ludicrous. Grillparzer, the poet, gives one of those examples, trivial in themselves, that often reveal character as by a lightning flash. He had gone in a hired carriage, he says, to visit the composer, and to discuss with him an opera-libretto. Beethoven accompanied him back to the city gate. "As he left the carriage," says Grillparzer, "I noticed a bit of paper lying on the seat which he had just vacated. I thought that he had forgotten it and beckoned him to come back; but he shook his head and with a loud laugh, as at the success of a ruse, he ran the faster in the opposite direction. I unrolled the paper and it contained exactly the amount of the carriage-hire, which I had agreed upon with the driver. His manner of life had so estranged him from all the habits and customs of the world that it probably never occurred to him that under other circumstances he would have been guilty of a gross offence. I took the matter as it was intended and laughingly paid my coachman with the money that had been given to me."

Such a man would naturally be intolerably meddlesome with persons whose affairs he considered himself concerned in, but whose point of view remained opaque to him. His two younger brothers' opinions of him would be worth hearing. The trip he made in 1812, already forty-two and famous, to Linz, where his brother Johann, then thirty-five, had established himself as an apothecary, was apparently undertaken with the express purpose of separating him from a woman with whom he was living. When his arguments (and probably threats) proved unavailing, he did not hesitate to make use of his reputation and influence against his brother.

"Excited by opposition," says Thayer, "Ludwig resorted to any and every means to accomplish his purpose. He saw the Bishop about it. He applied to the civil authorities. He pushed the affair so earnestly as at last to obtain an order to the police to remove the girl . . . if on a certain day she should still be found in Linz." Of course, as anyone less headstrong would have anticipated, Johann was

driven in his desperation into marrying her.
Twelve years later he says of his brother in a
conversation-book: "He always wants me to
come to his people—*non possibile per me.*"
"The obstacle," comments Thayer, "was Johann's wife, who had become one of 'his people'
because of the composer's interference with
Johann's private affairs at Linz."

Thus Beethoven's capriciousness increased as
it cut him off more and more from successful
interaction with the world, and his sense of
this opposition between his "me" and his milieu became exaggerated, pathological. As
in most eccentric and solitary people there grew
up in him a complicated mechanism of "rationalisation," in which self-respect is guarded by
the attribution of all kinds of evil to others.
He was never tired of abusing the Viennese,
more than even their partiality for Rossini
and other frivolities would seem to justify.
"Everywhere in public," says Simrock, "Beethoven railed at Emperor Franz because of the
reduction of the paper money. 'Such a rascal
ought to be hanged to the first tree,' said he.
But he was known and the police officials let
him do as he pleased." His idealisation of the
English was another obsession. This had the

small basis of rational justification that London had ordered works from him; but on this foundation he had reared a myth of English perfection, evidently largely elaborated as a "contrast effect" to set off the blackness of Vienna—another process familiar to pathologists. One Stumpff quotes him as saying in 1824, almost at the end of his life: "England stands high in culture. In London everybody knows something and knows it well; but the man of Vienna can talk only of eating and drinking, and sings and pounds away at music of little significance or of his own making." The animus behind this on the part of Beethoven, who had never been in London, is only too evident.

Thus did Beethoven remain to the end of his days, in all social contacts, essentially an undisciplined child: petulant, obstinate, unreasonable, thoughtless, naïve, unjust, selfish, unreliable—and yet in spite of all somehow lovable. Thayer's supreme merit, perhaps, is that he so reveals him, with all his faults clearly drawn, and not a jot abated, and yet the final result living, human, deeply appealing. Take, as a last instance, before passing to the musical aspect of the picture, Beethoven's love affairs. These, like everything else about him, have been idealised out of all resemblance to life by the earlier biographers. Even Philip Hale, not often a sentimentalist, cannot resist the seduction of the Beethoven myth, and writes: "There is no proof that he was ever under the spell of an unworthy passion. In an age when unlimited gallantry was regarded as characteristic of a polished gentleman, Beethoven was pure in speech and in life." Thayer reaches a contrary conclusion.

"Spending his whole life," he says, "in a state of society in which . . . the moderate gratification of the sexual was no more discountenanced than the satisfying of any other natural appetite—it is nonsense to suppose that Beethoven could have Puritanic scruples on that point. Those who have had occasion and opportunity to ascertain the facts, know that he did not, and are also aware that he did not always escape the common penalties of transgressing the laws of strict purity." Sir George Grove, even more specific, states that the deafness was due to degeneration and paralysis of the auditory nerves, especially that of the right ear—"probably the result of syphilitic affections at an early period of his life."

247

Beethoven was evidently as much a creature of impulse—though his impulses were never low or perverse—in this as in other matters. One of his friends records that when they met a pretty girl on the street, Beethoven would turn and stare after her, and if rallied by the friend would laugh. In 1800 there lived near him a peasant and his remarkably beautiful daughter, neither of them of good reputation. Beethoven was greatly captivated by her and was in the habit of stopping to gaze at her when he passed by where she was at work in farmyard or field. Once when her father was arrested for brawling, Beethoven tried to obtain his release. The story ends characteristically: "Not succeeding, he became angry and abusive, and in the end would have been arrested for his impertinence, but for the strong representations made by some who knew him, of his position in society, and of the high rank, influence, and power of his friends." In a letter of 1822 Beethoven mentions that two singers had called on him and asked to kiss his hands: "But as they were very pretty I suggested that they kiss my lips." Yet we must remember also the aspirations that always struggled in his instinct-ridden heart. He once said that he could never have written an opera on a text like Mozart's "Don Giovanni," and his own "Fidelio" is an inspiring picture of faithful love in marriage. In one of those old *Tagebuchs* to which he entrusted such an incongruous mass of plans for works, reflections, and soliloquies, we find the sentence: "Sensual enjoyment without a union of souls is bestial and will always remain bestial; after it, one experiences not a trace of noble sentiment, but rather regret." Alas, how much nobility there was in Beethoven that had never found through discipline its path into reality!

But in one field this much-suffering spirit was not baffled, and exasperated, and thrown back on himself; in one field he had found, from his earliest years, discipline and the freedom it gives; he could forget himself completely, because he had attained objective and completely successful activity, in his music. Beethoven enduring discipline!—it is a paradox, but in this one field it is the truth. To it his biographers have hardly done sufficient justice, perhaps because it is not so picturesque as his restiveness in ordinary life. His Sketch-books, to be sure, edited by Nottebohm, have long afforded extraordinary witness to his indefatigable search

for perfection: there are six large sketches, for
example, and many smaller fragments, for the
opening section of the Eroica Symphony.
Thayer gives further evidence. After men-
tioning that the melody to the "Opferlied" was
written out in full six times, he remarks:

"Absolute correctness of accent, emphasis,
rhythm—of prosody, in short—was with him
a leading object; and various papers, as well as
the Conversation Books, attest his familiarity
with metrical signs and his scrupulous obedi-
ence to metrical laws. . . . The sketches for
the conclusion of the Quintet fugue . . . are
mixed with notes from Bach and others showing how zealous were his studies in the form
at that time."

When he was working on the Great Mass in
D he wrote in the *Tagebuch:* "In order to
write true church music . . . look through all
the monastic church chorals and also the
strophes in the most correct translations and
perfect prosody in all Christian-Catholic psalms
and hymns generally." Thayer mentions that
he devoted five years to the composition of this
work, and "made so many changes in the
tympani part of the *Agnus Dei* that he wore a
hole in the very thick paper, his aim being,

apparently, by means of a vague rhythm to suggest the distance of the disturbers of the peace." But what is even more remarkable is that Beethoven—Beethoven the impatient, Beethoven the proud, Beethoven who threw a badly-cooked stew at the head of the waiter— Beethoven could on occasion take criticisms from players. We are told, indeed, that he "usually resented advice, then acted on it" (the "me" sense intruding even between him and his music), but sometimes he even forgot to resent it. Wegeler observes of the string quartet of players of early Vienna days, headed by Schuppanzigh, "Beethoven always listened with pleasure to the observations of these gentlemen," and records that it was at the suggestion of one of them, the violoncellist Kraft, that he changed the time-signature of the finale of the Trio, Opus 1, No. 3, from 4-4 to 2-4. It is true that he would not lower the voice parts in the Mass even though "Unger called him a 'tyrant over all the vocal organs' to his face." But he had lost his hearing and could hardly judge the justice of the criticism. Thayer specifically says: "The consequences of his obduracy were not realised by Beethoven at the concert, for though he stood among the

251

performers and indicated the *tempo* at the beginning of each movement he could not hear
the music except with his mental ear."

Beethoven had always been happiest when
absorbed in music: "I am never alone," he
notes in the *Tagebuch,* "when I am alone."
"You ask me where I get my ideas," he said
to Schloesser. "They come unsummoned, directly, indirectly—I could seize them with my
hands out in the open air; in the woods; while
walking; in the silence of the night; early in
the morning; incited by moods which are translated by the poet into words, by me into tones
—they sound and roar and storm about me
until I have set them down in notes." His
concentration was such that he composed part
of a march while giving Förster a lesson. He
usually only sketched his own parts in his en-
semble-compositions, playing them from memory. Amenda relates that one evening when
Beethoven had improvised he said to him: "It
is a great pity that such glorious music is born
and lost in a moment." "Whereupon B.:
'There you are mistaken; I can repeat every
extemporization'; and he sat down and played
it again without a change." This absorption
in music, in connection with which there are of

course countless tales of his absent-mindedness, so grew upon him that towards the end he lived hardly at all in this world of space and time of which he could make so little, he retired more and more to that other world he could control."

"Towards the end of August (1819)," narrates Schindler, "accompanied by Horsalka I arrived at the master's home in Mödling. It was four o'clock in the afternoon. As soon as we entered we learned that in the morning both servants had gone away, and that there had been a quarrel after midnight which had disturbed all the neighbors, because as a consequence of a long vigil both had gone to sleep and the food which had been prepared had become unpalatable. In the living room, behind a locked door, we heard the master singing parts of the fugue in the Credo—singing, howling, stamping. After we had been listening a long time to this almost awful scene, and were about to go away, the door opened and Beethoven stood before us with distorted features. He looked as if he had been in mortal combat with the whole host of contrapuntists, his everlasting enemies. His first utterances were confused. . . . Then he reached the day's happenings and . . . remarked, 'Pretty doings these! Everybody has run away and I haven't had anything to eat since yesterday!' "

How far was Beethoven himself conscious of the paradox of his nature? How far did he realise that those native impulses of his, so generous, so noble, so magnanimous as we see them in the ebullitions of his letters, in the touching prayers and *vade mecums* of the *Tagebuch,* and above all in the sublime contemplations of the later sonatas and quartets—how far did he realise that in the actual world they were for ever doomed to the fatal obstruction of his indiscipline? We can only guess from a few scattered jottings. In the *Tagebuch* of 1817, after writing, evidently with his nephew Karl in mind, "He who wishes to reap tears should sow love," suddenly he seems to see himself clearly, and cries: "There is no salvation for you except to go away, only thus can you swing yourself up to the summits of your art again, while here you are sinking into vulgarity." In a letter we find an even more general statement, in the words: "For Beethoven can write, thank God, though he can do nothing else in this world." The rest is in his music.

254

HOW BEETHOVEN WORKED

WHAT a magnificent subject Beethoven would be for a thoroughgoing psychoanalysis, and how many sentimental idealisations of him, repeated *ad nauseam* in all the books, such an analysis would explode! Even so able a writer as Ernest Newman hardly more than scratches the surface.[1] His general view is the one now widely accepted, that Beethoven, constantly balked in his relations with the actual world through his lack of any discipline such as could have fitted him to deal with it successfully, was thrown back upon the world of music, wherein discipline had given him mastery and the sense of power. "The only real world for him," he says, "was that of music; it puzzled and fretted him that the world that other men called real did not proceed upon the same lofty and simple principles as that other." And later: "Even the bitterness died out of his hypochondria as he retired more and more within himself, giving up as

[1] "The Unconscious Beethoven," by Ernest Newman, Alfred A. Knopf.

hopeless the attempt to reconcile the world within him and the world without." Newman believes that in his last years, giving up as insoluble the riddle of the outer world, Beethoven attained a "spiritual transfiguration," and that "when life ceased to draw its puzzling zigzags across his simple spirit, something of the inner light shone through the rugged, fissured rock that was the outer man." Everyone must agree that this happened who has listened understandingly to the later quartets and sonatas, to the Adagio of the Ninth Symphony, to the Benedictus of the Mass in D. But *how* it happened still remains a mystery.

As one would expect from a writer so well informed, so realistic, and so courageous as Newman, he gives short shrift to some of the time-honored superstitions about Beethoven. Refreshing is his refusal to accept "Fidelio" with the undiscriminating admiration of those whose musical judgment is affected by their moral edification over the libretto, or to be hypnotised by the humanitarian uplift of the Ode to Joy into ignoring the inferiority of the last movement of the Ninth Symphony to the other three. Enlightening are his reinterpretations of familiar facts of the composer's life in the light of recent psychology. He shows, for instance, that Beethoven's well-known hatred of loose women, far from being the rational and edifying evidence of moral principle it has been considered by superficial sentimentalists, was irrational, hysterical, almost mad—was, in short, a phobia, due to his unconscious association of sexual irregularities with the venereal disease which in his case they had led to, and with the terrible affliction of deafness which that had brought in its train. Such analysings-out of the automatisms in Beethoven's mind make us sensible of the human struggle of his life, and reduce him from a heroic statue, larger than life-size, to a real man, making him more lovable and truly admirable in the process.

The second part of the book, dealing with The Composer, is at once the most valuable and the most unsatisfactory: valuable because it discusses provocatively many curious features of Beethoven's actual creative process; unsatisfactory because it brings these considerations to no definite focus, and even uses its fundamental conceptions inconsistently—taking "unconscious," for instance, sometimes in the bad sense of mechanical or automatic and sometimes in the good sense of broad, free, and profound. One gets no definite ideas from this half of the book, and doubts if the author himself has any; yet it raises no end of fascinating problems, and is one of the most suggestive treatments of the mental processes of a composer.

The first half of it is taken up in showing, by a singularly thorough examination of the slow movements of Beethoven's Sonatas and other works, that he is subject to an "obsession," a figure of three notes rising in the diatonic scale, which flood up from his unconscious whenever he is in earnest mood. The documentation is impressive, but doubts arise. Are not the diatonic scale and the arpeggio the two fundamental melodic paths for all composers, at least through the eighteenth century, and is not rising movement instinctive with all melodists in moods of will, energy, earnestness, just as descending movement is instinctive in moods of melancholy and depression? On the whole, however, the point may be conceded as proved. Newman's conclusion from it seems to be that Beethoven is greater, more individual, in his fast movements than in his slow ones, that in these, being less alive, he sinks into automatisms, formulæ, such as these three-note figures and the like. He is thus using the "unconscious" in its æsthetically bad sense here.

Briefly the argument is that Beethoven began a great movement like the opening Allegro of the Eroica with a general scheme of the whole vaguely in his mind (rather than with definite melodies or themes, as we are told Mozart began) and then proceeded arduously to incarnate this scheme in appropriate themes. What we see in the sketch-books is the condensation into themes, sub-themes, transitions, developments, and so on of the dramatic or architectonic plan which was vaguely in his mind when he began. Here the author is considering the unconscious superior to the conscious. Now there is much to be said for this theory, but also much to be said against it.

The sketches often strikingly justify Newman's observation that Beethoven "was at first intent, now and then, not so much on hammering out his theme as on fixing proportions, modulation, and so on to his satisfaction; rather than hold up this part of his task in order to settle on the precise notes of a theme he would be content with a rough blocking out of this." Most composers will know by experience the necessity of such subordination of details to general design in a large work, and will sympathise with the comparison to the painter, who will "draw the rough outline of a head in its proper place, and splash in a suggestion of its value in the color scheme, leaving the filling-in of the features to a later time."

All this is not only exciting but highly needed by a generation inclined to neglect structure; yet one wonders whether the independence of structure upon idea cannot be exaggerated. In the nature of things we cannot know from Beethoven's sketch-books just the order in which scheme and theme appeared or alternated in his mind. But one suspects that theme determined scheme nearly or quite as much as scheme theme. "The thought of an end," shrewdly points out John Dewey, "is strictly correlative to perception of means and methods. Only when and as the latter becomes clear during the serial process of execution does the project and guiding aim and plan become evident and articulated. In the full sense of the word, a person becomes aware of what he wants to do and what he is about only when the work is actually complete." Possibly this

is overstatement in the opposite direction; but
one cannot fancy Beethoven's getting very far
with the Eroica, for instance, without the hammer strokes of that E flat major theme to
pound his mind to incandescence. Newman,
by the way, who is an incorrigible program-
matist, says that the famous conflict of dominant harmony in the violins with tonic harmony in the horn at a highly imaginative moment is unquestionably programmatic, that it
has a "symbolic significance." Does not this
illustrate the dangers of estimating poetic and
literary schemes generally at more than their
due importance? Beethoven might have
thought of an imaginary conflict, in the ab-
stract, till all was blue, without producing
anything worth discussing. But once he had a
theme like that, with its insistence on the tonic
harmony of E flat, all he had to do, and all he
tried to do (as Newman himself shows from
the sketches), was to put it into conflict with
dominant harmony to get one of the greatest
effects to be found anywhere in music. In
short, the conflict was a musical, not a poetic
one, and could not arise in his mind until the
theme afforded the ground of it.

So even if scheme was more important to

Beethoven, so dramatically minded, than it was to the lyrical Mozart (since structure is essential to drama) it is possible that scheme and theme are more reciprocally related than Newman leads us to suppose. It is possible that they grow up alternatively, or even simultaneously, in the composer's mind, and that neither one of them is entitled to creative priority.

BEETHOVEN'S HUMOR

HUMOR is a quality that ranges all the way from the cheap and somewhat cruel amusement we feel in seeing someone have his hat blown off, or run for and just miss a train, or take a sudden seat on an icy pavement, or in short in any way get "in a fix," to the sublime sense of subtle and ordinarily unnoticed incongruities or hidden similarities of a Shakespeare or a Meredith, or of the Beethoven of many passages in the symphonies. Beethoven, like Shakespeare, is so broad and rich a human personality that on the one hand he can sympathise with the lowest and coarsest clownishness, and on the other can reveal in a lightning flash of genius identities forever hidden from literal or prosaic minds. And while musical humor, like all other musical qualities, exists in a world by itself, a world incommensurable with our ordinary one,—the world of music—so that it is impossible to translate musical humor into ordinary humor, or indeed to express it in any save musical terms, yet there is nevertheless such a deep-lying similarity between the musical and the non-musical manifestations of a great and highly individual character like Beethoven's that familiarity with his daily life as it is revealed in such a book as Thayer's monumental biography, undeniably gives us many clues to the most startling peculiarities of the symphonies.

That comparatively low form of humor which enjoys seeing people "in a fix" (or even, and perhaps more, enjoys putting them there) was an essential ingredient of the impish, mischievous side of Beethoven. Of a set of variations he wrote at the time of his first arrival in Vienna and great fame there as a pianist, he writes to a friend: "I never would have composed a thing of the kind had I not often observed that here and there in Vienna there was somebody who, after I had improvised of an evening, noted down many of my peculiarities, and made parade of them next day as his own. Foreseeing that some of these things would soon appear in print, I resolved to anticipate them. Another reason I had was to embarrass the local pianists. Many of them are my deadly enemies, and I wanted to revenge myself on them, knowing that once in a while somebody would ask them to play the variations and they would make a sorry show with them." As with the pianists, so with the singers; and since singers are apt to be both stupider and more self-complacent than instrumentalists, they must have been fair game for Beethoven's malice. Such for instance was the tenor who sang the rôle of Pizarro in "Fidelio," Sebastian Meier, a brother-in-law of Mozart. To cure him of his conceit, Beethoven wrote a passage in Pizarro's air where the violins play repeatedly notes just a half-tone, or "minor second," away from those the singer is required to take, thus pulling him off the pitch. It must have been like walking on a shelving icy sidewalk, trying to keep out of the gutter. "Don Pizarro," we are told, "was unable with all his gesticulation and writhing to avoid the difficulty, the more since the mischievous players maliciously emphasised the minor seconds by accentuation." At last, goaded to rage by their laughter, he turned upon Beethoven, shouting: "My brother-in-law would never have written such damned nonsense."

The laughter of Beethoven's players was likely to be short-lived, however. He was merciless in the difficulties he expected them to master, and once, when a cellist told him a passage did not "lie well," he replied curtly, "It *must* lie well." Dragonetti, most famous of contrabassists, once delighted the composer by playing with him on the contrabass the cello part of his sonata, Opus 5, No. 2. "Beethoven played his part with his eyes immovably fixed on his companion, and in the finale, where the arpeggios occur, was so delighted that at the close he sprang up and threw his arms around both player and instrument. The unlucky contrabassists of orchestras had frequent occasion during the next few years to know that this new revelation of the powers and possibilities of their instrument to Beethoven was not forgotten." The only part of this story that does not bear internal evidence of its truth is the picture of Beethoven embracing at one and the same time a contrabassist and a contrabass— Beethoven, who was not only short and stocky in build but physically so awkward that in spite of his splendid sense of rhythm he could never dance, constantly dropped things, such as his ink-bottle into his piano, and usually cut himself on the rare occasions when he shaved. Here is part of a contemporary account of his conducting: "He used to suggest a *diminuendo* by crouching down more and more, and at a *pianissimo* he would almost creep under the desk. When the volume of sound grew, he rose up also, and with the entrance of the power of the band would stand upon his toes, and waving his arms, seemed about to soar upwards to the skies. . . . When things went to pieces, particularly in the scherzos of his symphonies at a sudden or unexpected change of rhythm, he would shout with laughter and say he had expected nothing else, but was reckoning on it from the beginning; he was almost childishly glad that he had been successful in 'unhorsing such excellent riders.' "

To listen sympathetically to such a movement as the Scherzo of his Second Symphony is almost to see his orchestra before us, with him grimacing and gesticulating at it, exploding in hoarse laughter when some instrument failed of its entrance. The movement is written on a simple theme of three rising notes—"*Do, re, mi*"—tossed about in successive measures all over the orchestra: sometimes given to only the violins, sometimes to two horns, sometimes to the whole band. The time is impetuous, there is no chance to prepare for your dive, you

267

must jump in when your turn comes, and sink or swim. And woe to the man that was wanting when Beethoven was ready for him. Scattered all through the nine symphonies, particularly in the scherzos and the finales, are similar effects of contrast and surprise: sudden alternations of very loud and very soft; violent dislocations of accent, such as in the first movement of the Eroica become fairly frenetic, and must have horrified early listeners accustomed to the decorum of Haydn and Mozart; the systematic dislocations known as "syncopations," highly whimsical in such a movement as the Minuet of the Fourth Symphony; and shifts of whole groups of notes in their relation to the measure such as appear first in the slow movement of the Second Symphony and attain great boldness of distortion in the famous "Metronome" movement of the Eighth. Such things, brilliant and delightful as they are, are only a step above mere physical animal spirits, naughty-boyish pranks, and have been distasteful to some highly refined natures like Chopin, who disliked what he called Beethoven's "roughness."

More intellectual is that playing with hidden tone-relationships which is so frequent in

268

all the symphonies, and indeed in everything Beethoven wrote. This again takes place on various levels, a comparatively low one being a mere toying with surface similarities akin to punning with words (it is worth noting that Beethoven was an inveterate punster in his letters). A good instance of such playing with the various possible significances of one tone occurs at the beginning of the development of the themes in the first movement of Symphony VIII, which is especially full of humor of all kinds, which Beethoven affectionately called his "Little One," and in which what he described as his "unbuttoned mood" prevails throughout. Three times does the bassoon sound the same fragment of four notes, but each time other instruments enter with a commentary which alters their meaning and orients them in a new direction: it is as if we added different chemicals to three test-tubes full of an innocent-looking transparent liquid, and with each produced some novel and strikingly unexpected reaction. . . . Or take the famous C sharp in the theme of the Eroica. Beethoven originally uses it simply to obscure a little his tonality and avoid too square-cut an effect. But having once introduced it, his mind plays with its possibilities in his tenaciously logical way, and three hundred and ninety-six measures or six minutes and a half later he reintroduces it, deflects it in a new direction by making a musical *double entendre,* and so arrives at the key he wants for the statement of his theme by the solo horn! . . . There is another famous C sharp in the symphonies: the one in the finale of the Eighth. Twice, at considerable distances apart, the merriment is interrupted by the bold intrusion of a wholly irrelevant C sharp, as gaunt and inexorable as the unbidden wedding guest. Twice the merriment overbears it and it is swept away, apparently ineffectual. But the third time it is more insistent; it repeats itself commandingly, and presently pulls the whole orchestra bodily into a new key (F sharp minor) and sets it dancing there more frenetically than ever. What an imagination, to make the significance of a single note shape a whole movement!

Indeed, a creative and untrammelled imagination, capable of remarking and delighting in not only all those incongruities that are lost upon the literal-minded man, the slave of his habits, and thus of revelling in that irresponsible confrontation of incommensurables which

we call humor, but also the likenesses deep hidden under the surface of things through which
the ordinary man never penetrates, and thus
of discovering beauty in the commonest things,
jewels in muck-heaps,—such a creative imagination is the source of all that is greatest in art.
And Beethoven had such an imagination as few
have had it. Few have equalled him in the
power of thematic development, of making
much from little, generating undreamed-of results from simple premises, and he is probably
the greatest of all writers of variations. Varia-
tion-making is nothing but the elaboration of
the associations of a subject or theme, associations made often over chasms of apparent difference that only the spark of genius
can overleap. This is why the subject itself that is varied is so unimportant and may
be so trivial: it is the boldness, rightness,
and richness of the associations that fascinate
us.

Here again the Beethoven of the letters is
the same man as the composer of the symphonies. When a singer was to present an aria
from "Fidelio" in concert, Beethoven was wor-
ried lest the dramatic effect should be lost, and
wrote a letter we may entitle

Variations on a Curtain
(New Year's Day, 1814)

"All would be well if there were but a curtain, without it the Air will fall through. Only today do I learn this from S. and it grieves me—let there be a curtain even if it be only a bed-curtain—only a sort of screen which can be removed for the moment, a veil. There must be something; the Air is too dramatic, too much written for the theatre, to be effective in a concert; without a curtain or something of the sort all of its meaning will be lost!—lost!—lost! To the devil with everything!

"Hangings!!! or the Air and I will hang tomorrow. Farewell in the New Year, I press you as warmly to my heart as in the old—with or without curtain."

As in words, so in tones: the subject mattered little, if only the imagination were ready to illuminate it. He would improvise on any theme given him by anyone; on one occasion at a quartet party in Vienna he picked up a second violin part lying on a desk, chose a phrase or two, and entranced the company with what it suggested to him. Was there ever another composer who could make the finale of a great symphony like the Eroica from a comparatively trivial bit of his own ballet music, using sometimes its melody, and sometimes nothing but its bass! When he was writing the Seventh Symphony, he was also making some arrangements of Scottish folk-songs for an Edinburgh publisher. From one of them he took a phrase from the quite commonplace interlude for piano between stanzas, changed it from 6-8 time to 2-4, increased its pace, and made from it the breath-taking finale of the symphony, one of his greatest conceptions. The sublime passage that leads from the scherzo to the finale of the Fifth Symphony is made from a simple rhythmic figure tapped by the drum and a hardly more complicated violin melody. The lovely ending of the slow movement of the Fourth Symphony, as romantic as "As You Like It," takes much of its character from a simple tapping of kettledrums. Thus can genius build beauty out of sticks and stones, and throw over the commonest everyday objects "the light that never was on sea or land."

BEETHOVEN: 1827-1927

*(Centennial Essay written in 1927 to com-
memorate the one hundredth anniversary
of Beethoven's death)*

I

HOW many of the works of art we are
producing today are likely to last out a
century? How many of them will be vigorously alive in the year 2027? . . . When we
reflect that a century ago, in 1827, when
Beethoven died, our modern industrial world
was just beginning—that he traveled in horse-
coaches, worked of an evening by candle-light,
and wrote his symphonies with goose-quills—
we realise that to survive so many changes his
work must possess an extraordinary vitality.
And even though the changes of the coming
century are likely to be more psychological than
material, it is a sobering thought to ask ourselves how many of *our* works, whether material or spiritual, are sufficiently alive to have
a chance of surviving them?

Beethoven's last intelligible words, whis-

pered two days before he died on March 26,
1827, are said to have been: "Applaud, friends,
the comedy is finished." But if the comedy, or
tragi-comedy, of Ludwig van Beethoven's
troubled existence in the flesh was indeed drawing to a close, the great drama to which it was
only the uneasy prologue—the drama of the
gradual permeation of the entire world by his
glorious music, was just beginning. That
drama is still enacting. "An immortal like
Shakespeare," says Samuel Butler, "knows
nothing of his own immortality . . . when it
is in its highest vitality, centuries, it may be,
after his apparent death." Such is the case
of Beethoven: his truest and happiest life is
that of which he is himself entirely unconscious, that which is now spread over the world.
Trivial details often suggest great truths.
Beethoven, physically awkward, could never
learn to cut for himself the goose-quills with
which he wrote. He formed the habit therefore of sending hurried notes to a friend of his,
one Zmeskall, whenever he needed pens, and
this Zmeskall, aware of the possible future
value of these scrawls, saved everyone of
them, from the merest line to the whimsical
punning letters into which Beethoven expanded

when he was in a good humor, joking his friend in every way that occurred to him, and even inventing absurd nicknames for him such as "Baron Muckcart-driver," "His Well Well Highest and Bestborn," and "His Zmeskallian Zmeskallity." Well, these scraps are now scattered, says Thayer, in his biography of Beethoven, "in all civilised lands as autographs." We pride ourselves, in our age of invention and material luxury, on the handsome typewriters with which we have replaced the miserable quills that gave poor Beethoven so much trouble. Let us not deceive ourselves. In 2027 most of our handsome typewritten letters will long have rotted away; but Beethoven's scrawls will still be carefully guarded under glass in the libraries. Such is the preservative power of genius.

II

Born in 1770 at Bonn on the Rhine, Ludwig van Beethoven moved in his early twenties to Vienna, the Austrian capital, and spent the rest of his life there. The general lines of his work had been already determined by his great predecessors, Haydn (1732-1809) and Mozart (1756-1791), whose traditions he closely followed. On the whole a smaller proportion of his work than of theirs was for voices; and while he wrote one famous opera —"Fidelio," a great Mass, and many songs, he concentrated his best efforts on pure instrumental music, and brought it to a higher power of expression than it had ever reached before. In at least four departments of instrumental music Beethoven achieved supreme mastery. Yet in all these he was only following the lead of earlier composers, and he did not so much invent new methods as infuse new power, breadth, profundity, and variety into those already familiar.

The first department is that of music for piano alone, to which Beethoven contributed his thirty-two Piano Sonatas, among them such well-known favorites as the "Moonlight," the "Waldstein" and the "Appassionata." The second department is that of chamber music, or music for the private drawing room as distinguished from the concert hall, though nowadays it is played in small concert halls as well as in private houses. Beethoven wrote many fine sonatas for violin and piano (the so-called "Kreutzer Sonata" is a famous example) and several for violoncello and piano, as well as trios for all three instruments, and indeed quartets, quintets, and sextets. One of his early sextets is of that sort of merely pretty music he later came to hate as having no expressive reason for being; and when he was shown it in later years, he exclaimed: "Oh, Beethoven, what an ass you were!" The most beautiful type of chamber music was that which had been worked out by Haydn and Mozart for a quartet of stringed instruments,—two violins, a viola, and a violoncello; and to this Beethoven contributed a series of sixteen String Quartets which cover his whole active life and contain much of his most beautiful, characteristic, and profound music.

The third department is music for orchestra. Here again Haydn and Mozart had prepared the way by fixing the constitution of the orchestra in four essential groups: wood-wind instruments, brass instruments, percussion instruments, and strings; and by writing many symphonies (Mozart wrote forty-nine and Haydn no less than a hundred and twenty-five) in which the methods of Beethoven's nine symphonies were clearly and fully anticipated. They also wrote pieces for orchestra having only a single movement instead of the four pieces or movements found in a symphony, and called overtures. Beethoven wrote eleven Overtures, of which the best known are the "Egmont," "Coriolanus" and three Leonore Overtures. A fourth and last department is provided by the addition of solo instruments to the orchestra in pieces called "concertos." Beethoven wrote five Concertos for Piano and Orchestra (the last, called the "Emperor Concerto" is especially well known) and one splendid Concerto for Violin and Orchestra.

Beethoven also followed Haydn and Mozart closely, especially in his youth, in his methods of building up all these works. Thus of the four movements or separate pieces that usually made up a sonata, a quartet, or a symphony of any one of the three masters, the two middle movements are usually the simplest, and the most obviously derived from the two instinctive activities of human beings that underlie all music: dance and song. When we are serious or meditative, we instinctively sing: and the composer only needs to elaborate our songs a little, and to build them up by natural contrasts into effective pieces, to get the slow movements which Beethoven wrote so incom-

279

parably. In one of the earliest of these, the Largo of the Seventh Piano Sonata, Opus 10, No. 3, we find those depths of contemplation, of earnest and noble feeling, that Beethoven knew so well how to open to us. The same methods had only to be extended by increasing experience of his art and enriched by deepening experience of life, to give us the marvellous profundities of the Adagios of the Quartet in E flat, Opus 127, and the Ninth Symphony.

And when we are gay, we dance. To that fact we owe the presence of the minuet in the classic sonata and symphony. With Haydn and Mozart this is a stately, courtly dance, in a dignified three-beat time. Beethoven, even in his first symphony, makes it more headlong, more full of animal spirits, and by the time he gets to the third or Eroica Symphony, he coins a new name for it ("scherzo," pronounced skairtso, an Italian word meaning "joke"), and fills it to the brim with the humor of giants and gods. Nothing is greater in Beethoven than his great scherzos, just as nothing is greater in Shakespeare than his clown scenes. And their variety is equally surprising. In the Fifth Symphony there is a sense of mystery, almost of dread, in the mood of the scherzo;

as Berlioz said, "It is as fascinating as the gaze of a mesmeriser." In the Sixth or Pastoral Symphony, a picture of country life, the scherzo naturally enough takes the form of a merry but somewhat primitive dance of peasants, with the ludicrous incident of the old bassoon player who has only three good notes on his instrument, and has to wait for the music to come round to them. The scherzos of the Seventh and Eighth Symphonies are perfect carnivals of whimsical irresponsible rhythm, and that of the Ninth is a sort of super-scherzo for super-men.

In the first and last movements of a symphony we have the same elements of song and of dance that make up the slow movements and the minuets or scherzos, but combined here in more elaborate and complex schemes of design. Indeed, the first movement is the one in which that element of far-flung and highly-organised design that there always is in the greatest music, and that made someone speak of architecture as "frozen music," manifests itself most completely; and as Beethoven was as incomparable in the logic, concentration, and scope of his mind as in the depth and variety of his expression, his first movements

are the supreme masterpieces of his art. They
are modelled on the general lines of Haydn
and Mozart in consisting first of the presenta-
tion of three characteristic melodies or themes,
then of their development, and then of their
final summing up in simple restatement; the
three sections being called respectively: Expo-
sition, Development, and Recapitulation. To
these Beethoven often adds a slow Introduction to prepare the hearer for what is to come,
and a Coda or tail-piece to clinch the final
impression. Such a movement as the opening
Allegro of the Eroica Symphony, gigantic in
proportions yet as clear and justly balanced in
ultimate effect as the Parthenon, is a masterpiece of musical architecture which gives one a
new respect for the capacities of the human
mind. And the finale of the same symphony,
a set of variations on a theme from some ballet
music of Beethoven's, is a revelation of what a
master-mind can do with apparently unpromising material.

Beethoven has been said by a discerning
critic to mark the happy moment in musical
history when there was "a perfect balance of
expression and design." Before him expression had not quite reached its maximum free-

dom; after him it got out of hand and few modern works are as completely and powerfully organised as his. His later piano sonatas and quartets, and his greatest symphonies such as the Eroica, the Fifth, and the Ninth, are as beautiful and permanently satisfying in their shape, in their organisation, as they are profound and poignant in their communication of emotion. The vicissitudes of artistic fashions can hardly permanently affect such work; in our moments of reaction we may disparage it as "romantic" or even "sentimental," as our ultra-modern ironists have been doing lately; but their disillusion will pass, and as long as human nature loves beauty and responds to feeling, it will in the long run love Beethoven.

III

In what, then, does Beethoven's genius consist? Such a question, irresistible as it is to ask, seems to be impossible to answer. Whole libraries of books have been written about Beethoven: about the traditions he inherited from earlier workers on whom he formed his style; about his immediate blood-inheritance from grandfather and father, both professional musicians, one a man of sterling character and great influence in his community, the other a drunkard and ne'er-do-well; about his health, his nervous irritability, his perversities and eccentricities, his deafness; about his dealings with the wealthy noblemen who helped him make his way in Vienna; about his reading, his philosophy and religion, his eating and drinking, his business dealings, not always scrupulously honest—in short, about every minutest fact of his life, down to the very goose-quills, as we have seen, with which he wrote. And yet all this discussion has not solved the mystery of his power. There are, however, certain things about him well worth observing—things interesting in themselves, things important for us to notice if we wish to prepare the ground for any new Beethovens that may arise, and things that help us to understand his music (and all music) more fully, and to enjoy it more keenly.

First of all, music was to Beethoven no agreeable pastime, no pleasant diversion. It was his life. So absorbed in it was he that all other things seemed to him of little importance. Often, when composing, he forgot to sleep and even to eat. In the early days of his mingling with the court society of Vienna, he bought himself a horse, but promptly forgot that he owned it, so that the poor animal nearly died of starvation. As he took his morning walk around the ramparts of the city, half running in his excitement, he would sing his melodies aloud, talk to himself, gesticulate, sometimes shout. Coming from a walk in the rain into a Viennese drawing-room, he would shake himself like a mastiff, spattering with water his patient patrons. In later years, as he walked and composed at his brother's country estate, his wild gestures frightened a team of bullocks into running away. When composing, he hated to think of bothersome everyday matters, and in illness would take all his medicine for the week on Sunday morning. Hofel, a young painter, asked him to sit for his portrait. For five minutes he remained reasonably quiet; then springing up went to the piano and began to improvise. The servant advised Hofel to follow him there and continue his sketch at his leisure, since, he said, "his master had quite forgotten him and no longer knew that anyone was in the room." He worked as long as he wished and then departed without the slightest notice from Beethoven.

Again, although Beethoven as a skilled pianist was in demand in the drawing-rooms of Vienna, and although he took a perfectly simple and natural human delight in exhibiting his skill, the empty vanity of the virtuoso was far from him, and he never regarded music as a display any more than as a diversion. Mere prettiness was detestable to him. He was comparatively careless, says one of his piano pupils, "as to the right notes being played, but angry at once at any failure in expression or nuance; saying that the first might be an accident, but that the other showed want of knowledge, or feeling, or attention. Of a pianist who pretended to improvise something worth hearing, but played only brilliant runs and ornaments, he demanded rudely: "When are you going to begin?" In his own improvising, he cared little what theme he chose, taking any that was suggested, but brought out all its possibilities with such richness of imagination, such unexpected depth and beauty of expression, and such magnificent logic (as we see in his written works) that his hearers were often moved to tears. When this happened, he would laugh boisterously and rally them on their susceptibility. But he was pleased none the less, and indeed deeply moved himself: the antics were no doubt a means of getting down from sublimity to ordinary life again without too rude a shock.

So vital was expression to Beethoven that he spared himself no pains to perfect it. In this aspect of its painstaking art his work should be a particularly salutary lesson to our hasty, careless and superficial modern ways. His art was anything but half-baked and jerry-built as so much of ours is. He had the Ninth Symphony in mind twenty-five years. The melody of one of his songs he wrote out entire six times before he could get the accentuation of the words to suit him. Self-willed as he was in everyday life, he would take criticism from musicians far less gifted than himself when he saw a chance of deepening the expression of his music. After his deafness had become almost complete, four players were rehearsing his quartet in E flat. One of them advised that a slow passage he had placed near the end, marked *meno vivace* (less lively), should be omitted, as he thought it injured the effect. "Beethoven, crouched in a corner, heard nothing, but watched with strained attention. After the last stroke of the bows, he said laconically: 'Let it remain so,' went to the desks and crossed out the *meno vivace* in the four parts." [1]

In this picture of the deaf Beethoven conquering the tragic obstacle of his deafness by the greatness of his thought and the patient effort of his art there is something sublime. And this lesson of thought and patience triumphing over material obstacles is perhaps the greatest lesson of Beethoven's life to an age, like ours, enslaved to the material. It ought to be healthily humiliating to us to realise that for all our inventions, all our luxuries, all our "progress" as we like to call it, we cannot do even with our great modern orchestra what he did with his smaller orchestra, with its wind instruments unprovided with modern fingering systems and its brasses without valves. We accept so thoughtlessly the modern superstition that machinery is more important than thought, and with such disastrous results to our art. Mark Twain, writing to congratulate Walt Whitman on his seventieth birthday, exclaims: "What great births you have witnessed! The

[1] Thayer's Beethoven, III, 193. For further examples see the chapter on "Workmanship" in "Artistic Ideals," by the present writer.

288

steam press, the steamship, the steel ship, the railroad, the perfect cotton gin, the telegraph, the phonograph, photogravure, the electrotype, the gaslight, the electric light, the sewing machine and the amazing, infinitely varied, and innumerable products of coal tar, those latest and strangest marvels of a marvelous age." Well, Beethoven's age did not produce coal tar, but it produced the Fifth Symphony. And such a work of thought, however simple its material embodiment, is far more important to human happiness than "all these strangest marvels of a marvelous age," these coal-tar products of Mark Twain. A wiser observer of our American life, Thoreau, came nearer the truth when he said: "Our inventions are but improved means to an unimproved end. . . . We are eager to tunnel under the Atlantic and bring the old world some weeks nearer to the new; but perchance, the first news that will leak through into the broad flapping American ear will be that the Princess Adelaide has the whooping cough." One could not but remember Thoreau's prophecy recently when telephone conversation was established for the first time between London and New York, and they proceeded to exchange conventional platitudes over three thousand miles . . . Beethoven reversed the process. So crude were his horns and trumpets without valves that he was forced to put the passage for them in the Andante of the Fifth Symphony three times in the same key, and to give the horn call of the first movement, on its second appearance, to the highly inappropriate bassoons. Yet for these crude instruments Beethoven wrote—the Fifth Symphony. That is all we remember.

And so we are celebrating the vitality of this music that has lasted a century, and that will last many more. Beethoven was as fortunate in his personal gifts as we have seen him to be in his historical position. To the work that was ready for him to do he brought a rare normality and completeness of personality. Few composers have been so universal in their sympathies. No man was less snobbish, less what is called a "high-brow," than he. Daring as he was in discovering new beauty, mere novelty for itself, mere eccentricity, had no appeal to him, and it is amusing to reflect how many nine days' wonders he has survived. On the other hand there was nothing of the "low-brow" about him either; he had no patience with the triviality and platitude of what is called "popular music"—fortunately for us, for of the popular composers of his day not even the names are now remembered. No, Beethoven's music, like all good music, is for neither high-brows nor low-brows, but for all sincere and intelligent men and women. Hence we are honoring ourselves as well as him in celebrating this centenary. We are proclaiming that what we fundamentally and permanently like in music, what we can keep on liking for hundreds of years, is noble and deep feeling expressed in beautiful and enduring forms—and that such is the music of Beethoven.

BEETHOVEN: 1770-1920

(Written in 1920 to commemorate the one hundred and fiftieth anniversary of Beethoven's birth)

BORN a hundred and fifty years ago, Beethoven was never more alive than he is today. His life, now become unconscious, is immeasurably more widely diffused than when he was in the flesh. Wherever music is loved, he is at work. Samuel Butler, pointing out this centrifugal character of mental life, its beginning in a nucleus of personality like that which was born at Bonn on the Rhine, December 16, 1770, and slowly diffusing to the four corners of the earth an impersonal influence, drew vividly as a corollary his paradox that the best part of our life is unconscious. In Beethoven's case it was undeniably so: in his conscious life he was lonely, ill, deaf, misunderstood, harassed by a hundred limitations physical and mental; in his artistic life only did his great spirit soar free. And yet—"so nigh is grandeur to our dust"—his artistic life itself,

292

in which is his immortality, was the slow achievement of his mortal struggles, perfected painfully day by day through the conquest of imperfections, shining with a light which, however serenely luminous it may seem, was generated in the frictions of endless efforts of his indomitable will. This is what gives him his peculiar place in our imaginations: to every perceiving heart he becomes a symbol of our tragic humanity, which has to traverse pain to find happiness, and to which beauty is revealed only after far journeyings.

What was it in Beethoven that enabled him thus to find, amid all his struggles, confusions, and defeats, this path to true immortal life, this path which eluded so many more facile minds of his own and later days? What is it that keeps his music fresh long after that of his contemporary, Spohr, more famous than he in their day, has exhibited its pitiful weakness, long after most of that of the elegant Mendelssohn, of a later generation, seems in its jejune amiability hopelessly outmoded? Some will answer such questions by quoting Emerson's fine sentence: "The way to speak and write what shall not go out of fashion is to speak and write sincerely." No doubt Bee-

thoven's sturdy sincerity, verging often on
ferocious unconventionality, had a close causal
connection with the emotional power of his
work; no doubt in him as in all men, man and
artist, moral and æsthetic manifestation, were
in a deep sense one. But sincerity by itself
does not explain artistic power; the world is
full both of "mute inglorious Miltons" and of
competent artists who, while by no means
mute, are neither particularly glorious; in
short, as it has been well said: "Great music
is not the expression of great emotion, but the
great expression of emotion." Our question
resolves itself, then, to a more manageable
one, more manageable because, leaving moral
considerations on one side, it formulates itself
in purely æsthetic terms, namely: "How did
Beethoven achieve the great expression of emotion?" To this one would like to reply, tenta-
tively, "By concentration and elimination."

When, in Beethoven's final dropsical illness,
the doctors were tapping him for water, the
stricken Titan remarked grimly: "Better from
my belly than from my pen." The remark
illustrates his life-long contempt of the dilute,
the platitudinous, the conventional, the "bro-
midic," and suggests the earnestness of his

294

search for the opposite qualities, for distinctiveness, for characterisation, for the quintessential distillation of his thought, all his thought, and nothing but his thought. Into the polite eighteenth century symphonic world of Haydn and Mozart he bursts as he used to burst into the drawing-rooms of aristocratic Vienna on rainy days, shaking the water from him like a mastiff. He sweeps away the formulas, the *clichés*, those cadence figures of tonic and dominant that even Mozart tolerated, as a housewife sweeps away the cobwebs from a room long closed. He scraps all the old moulds. Every note has to stand the acid test of expressiveness. Is it expressive, does it characterise?—then let us use it, however harsh, ugly, or surprising. Is it merely pretty and unnecessary?—then away with it to the ash-bin! To a pianist who improvised such pretty ineptitudes Beethoven listened impatiently a moment or two, and then cried rudely, "When are you going to begin?"

It was this concentration on expression, far more than any limitation of sense, even after deafness had developed, that made him, as compared with Mozart, for example, so indifferent to sensuous charm of tone. Though both his orchestration and his writing for the piano frequently attain the greatest felicity of tone-quality, there are muddy basses in some of his sonatas, and his orchestra can hardly be said to have the silvery lightness, the magically right equilibrium of Mozart. On the other hand, he drives home his phrase with a relentlessness of emotional logic that makes Mozart seem like a care-free boy compared with an earnest man. Such a comparison has been made in detail by Sir Hubert Parry, in his "The Evolution of the Art of Music," between the treatment by the two masters of somewhat similar phrases, showing Mozart's charm, Beethoven's grim concentration. So intent was he on following out this emotional logic of his thought that questions of *timbre* seemed to him secondary. He was quite free of that morbid preoccupation with *timbre* of so many composers of today, who write to exploit the instruments rather than to make the instruments express their thoughts.

No, not only does Beethoven, whom the nervous agony of the process of composing often drove to shouting and stamping, lack the smiling ease of Mozart, but his music, full of mysterious shadows and strange lights, cloudy and stormy as a northern sky, has seldom a moment of the golden Italian sunshine that bathes the music of the other. It is by intensity of characterisation that his work is differentiated from all that went before it, and from most that has come after. He still remains unrivalled in the expressive use of all those devices, some of which he invented outright, others adapted and improved out of recognition from more timid talents: the gradual *crescendo* culminating not in loud but in unexpected soft; the long-maintained breathless *pianissimo;* sudden violent contrasts and dislocations, both of key and of rhythm; suspense in all its forms, and the arousal of expectation, sometimes to be fulfilled and sometimes to be pleasingly disappointed by the substitution of something more interesting; the subtle use of foils, pauses, and silences. And all this arsenal of weapons is used never loosely, but always with the nicest discrimination of the exact expressive aim to be achieved and the simplest way to achieve it. Each of Beethoven's symphonies, after the first two at any rate, which were student works, is like a plant grown out of a unique seed: every cell of it belongs to it, and to it alone; the themes, the transitions,

297

the modulations, the orchestration, the minutest inconspicuous ornament, are of a piece. Thus each symphony has, as few works in musical literature, its atmosphere, in which it is bathed, down to the last note: the third is heroic, the fourth romantic, the fifth tragic, the sixth pastoral and rustic, the seventh corybantic or bacchanalian, the eighth whimsical, and the ninth deeply humane and religious.

Let no one suppose that such concentration was easily attained. Had we no testimony from his contemporaries of his ravings and shoutings when composing, of his forgetfulness of meals and sleep, the evidence of those extraordinary sketch-books in which he hammered from refractory and often commonplace ideas his great themes would suffice to show us his command of that elimination of the inessential which every artist recognises as the price of vitality. Strange is it at first, and yet not on consideration, that one who could tolerate so little direction from his teachers, and of whom one of them said: "He has learnt nothing, and will never do anything in decent style," should yet willingly impose upon himself the severest of lifelong discipline. It was because he recognised that discipline, with the

deep respect it implies for the laws of nature—
a matter quite other than any man-made rules,
which Beethoven delighted to break—is the
indispensable means of mastery:

> "Upon his will he binds a radiant chain.
> For Freedom's sake he is no longer free."

And so Beethoven became a master, his
work lives, and his life widens into a mighty
stream.

EPILOGUE:
THREE RESTAURANTS

AMALFI: Easter Sunday.

THE South Italian is notoriously emotional and dramatic. It is natural to the Neapolitan to express his feelings with the voluptuous abandon of grand opera, and to forget them quickly after that purgative expression; so that when you get into one of a group of twenty small boats at Palermo, and find yourself at once, as it were, on a grand opera stage, surrounded by mad gesticulation and shouting addressed to no one in particular, amid vociferations of glee, fury, rage, and mortal bereavement, all of which pass off within a minute, you hardly know whether you are more amused or bewildered, "so different," as the Victorian English maiden lady said in emerging from the theater, is this highly charged Antony and Cleopatra atmosphere "from the home life of our own beloved Queen." Then, if you land at Naples, you get the same impression a little more intensified, from the mad antics, and to an Anglo-Saxon the equally mad subsidences and forgettings, of the cabmen and the *facchini*. A lira too little, a lira less than can be extracted by enacting battle, murder, and sudden death, is the signal for a brain storm that breaks into genial sunshine with the appearance of the coveted pennies. Neapolitans are avaricious, perhaps; perhaps they have to be; but they are artists not through necessity but by the grace of God.

To be convinced that they are musicians in the same way, you have only to forget the stereotyped statements of the books about "Italy, the sunny land of music," and to listen with open ears to such a group as we first heard in a café at luncheon in Pompeii. First of all, to an American, is the blessed relief of no machine-made noise, no hectic percussion, no ear-splitting, digestion-deranging impingement of metallic resonance. The guitar is the foundation. It gives a quiet permeating bass that reaches the farthest corners of the room without being loud three feet away, and of course it twangs the subordinate rhythm—the tum-tum after the first note—in the good old Rossini-Bellini-Donizettian manner. To it a first violin, at Pompeii, added the simple but often beautifully phrased melody, and a second violin, played with the self-effacing sense of ensemble of all true second players with the hearts of artists, gave a bit of shading just where it was needed, and merged at just the right moment into background. And a voice, too, of course, for the star numbers on the program, a baritone who went for the pitch like a bee for honey, and who never bawled or bellowed.

Such was the lay-out, and a better could not be devised for a room of medium size where people wish to talk and eat as well as listen, and do not need to have their ear-drums blown up by dynamite in order to forget how jaded they are. As for style, of course the pieces were so simple that any pedant would sneer at them, missing the point as pedants will—in harmony, for instance, hardly anything but tonic and dominant, and in phraseology usually resting content with the couplet. But not only were the phrases often beautiful, witty, or arresting in themselves, but they were delivered with a native sense of dramatic contrast and nuance that were irresistible. In particular one noticed sometimes an inset of two or three lines of breathless *pianissimo* of which the Flonzaley Quartet need not have been ashamed—neither in conception nor in execution. *Pianissimo* in a restaurant!—and it came off every time, because it was felt and imagined. This and the delicious rhythm, never coarse, never stereotyped, was what one carried away: and if in a Sousa march, played possibly in compliment to the many Americans "doing" Pompeii under the guidance of Messrs. Cook, there were places where the harmony was laughably too much for the resources of these unlettered men, one laughed, remembering Broadway, rather sorrily.

The second time we heard such a group was at dinner in a hotel in Naples. This time the music was more pretentious, and more commonplace. One of the singers was a lover of music. The other had a detestable tremolo, preferred "passion" to pitch, and was obviously singing for his public rather than for himself. This impression of an *entente cordiale* between sincere unschooled music and commercialised eclecticism has now been happily obliterated by the third and last group, warming the tail-end of a particularly rainy Easter Sunday on the spectacular but very stony cliffs of Amalfi with some genuine music again, as native as spaghetti.

This time, in addition to the two guitars and a mandolin, there was a curious instru-

303

ment, a large jar about a foot high and fat in proportion, called a "langella," into which a man blows, and which marks by the resonance of its air column the main accents: in short, that musical paradox and missing link, a wind percussion. At first one fancied it a true bass —a sort of grunt as of a sixteen-foot organ pedal, a bagpipe ground, or the pizzicato of a double-bass. But not at all. It recurred persistently wherever the music went, even when it changed key, and without any obtrusive effect of maladjustment. It came agreeably from the room at the end of the suite of dining rooms most removed from the musicians when its player, who was also treasurer of the band, was collecting contributions and demonstrating it to the curiosity of the guests. A wind-percussion: what nation but a naturally musical one would have devised such a polar contrast to the Frankensteins of "jazz"? It seemed to fill the very air with the rhythm, as if walls and ceiling responded to it, yet violated you no more than the gentle guitars with which it perfectly merged. Render unto Cæsar the things that are Cæsar's, and unto God the things that are God's. The razzle-dazzle for Broadway, and the langella for Amalfi.

And then, finally, there were our two gallant soloists, aged ten or twelve, gallant in
spirit, even if quailing a little in the flesh as
they stood on the landing of the stairway
where the black-robed monks once descended
in this old Capuchin monastery, and faced the
curious, amused, or indifferent guests, Americans who thought them picturesque, Germans
who thought them riff-raff, kindly but aloof
English in evening dress, in spite of the tem-
perature, who appeared not to think at all.
They sang in alternation, with a timid stiff bow
to begin with, stiff little well-learned gestures
of the hands, interrupted sometimes by wholly
spontaneous nose or head scratchings, and stiff
but slightly happier, more assured bows when
the end of the song came and they could retire
behind the mandolin-player, leader and cap-
tain. Their singing, too, was adorably un-
tutored, with a matter-of-fact detachment of
the last note of each phrase as if to say
"There! That's done!" and business-like tone-
production that was almost raucous in one of
them, but withal so full of gusto and so
squarely and triumphantly on the pitch that
criticism forgot itself, and music had its way.
There was all through it a conviction, for the

sympathetic listener, that what they had learned could not upset what they had not unlearned. They sang like birds, fledgling birds, birds with big heads and long necks and sparse pinfeathers, but after all birds. And it is better to be a very wobbly bird than the most perfect sixteen-cylinder calliope.